Brilliant Activities for Reading Fiction

Comprehension Activities for 7–11 Year Olds

May Stevenson

Brilliant Publications

If you and your class enjoy using the ideas in this book, you might be interested in the other books in the series:

Brilliant Activities for Reading Non-fiction   978-903853-46-7
Brilliant Activities for Persuasive Writing   978-903853-54-2

For more information on these and other books in the series, please contact us at the address given below.

Acknowledgements
The publishers and author are most grateful to Paula Goodridge for her excellent editing and comments.

Every effort has been made to try to trace the copyright holder of the poem "The seasons" on page 55. If anyone lets us know who the author of this poem is we will correct the mistake as soon as feasible.

Published by Brilliant Publications
Sales and despatch:
    BEBC Brilliant Publications
    Albion Close, Parkstone, Poole, Dorset BH12 3LL
    Tel: 0845 1309200 / 01202 712910
    Fax: 0845 1309300
    e-mail: brilliant@bebc.co.uk
    website: www.brilliantpublications.co.uk
Editorial and marketing:
    1 Church View, Sparrow Hall Farm, Edlesborough, Dunstable,
    Bedfordshire LU6 2ES

The name Brilliant Publications and its logo are registered trade marks.

Written by May Stevenson
Illustrated by Frank Endersby
Cover designed and illustrated by Lynda Murray
Copyright © May Stevenson 2006

ISBN: 978-1-903853-45-0

First published in 2006
10   9   8   7   6   5   4   3   2   1

Contents

Introduction

How to be Brilliant at Reading Fiction provides teachers with a wide selection of material for Key Stage 2 pupils to learn from and enjoy. Pupils are encouraged throughout to participate orally as well as in writing. All worksheets can be photocopied and most have several activities based on one theme.

All the activities are compatible with the Primary Literacy Strategy programmes of study.

The activities are suited for both independent and class work, depending on what the teacher considers appropriate. The contents page shows the variety of interesting themes used to fit in with the requirements of the National Curriculum.

Each section comprises a text which should be photocopied onto a separate sheet for ease of reading, and differentiated worksheets, and most sections have extension activities aimed at the more able readers. Extension activities give ideas to enhance certain aspects more thoroughly, giving teachers extra material for language teaching.

1. Fairy tale beginnings

Aim

The children should already be familiar with the stories of Cinderella, Goldilocks and the Three Bears, Pinocchio, Little Red Riding Hood and Sleeping Beauty. They will read and understand the beginning of each story. They will be able to recognize and locate words that are used to describe settings. They will be able to recognize speech marks as a method of telling us when people speak in stories.

Activities

a) Read the story beginnings on sheet **1a** as a class. Ask the pupils to find the phrase in each one which tells us when the story took place (e.g. "once upon a time"). Write the phrases on the board.

b) Look at story 1. Which words tell us that something nasty or dangerous might happen? Write the words on the board. Do the same for stories 2–4.

c) Divide the children into groups. Ask the children to decide which fairy tale each beginning is from. Lower ability pupils could be given a list of fairy tales to choose from (sheet **1b**). Discuss their answers.

d) As a class, look again at sheet **1a**. In the first story, what does Mother say to Little Red Riding Hood? How is this shown in the text? Point out the beginning and ending speech marks. Which words in the speech tell us that Grandmother is sad?

e) Tell the children that you are going to ask them to work independently to identify from which story some quotes come. They will also need to think of other things people in the story might have said and write these correctly using speech marks. Sheet **1c** is for the less able. Sheet **1d** is for the more able (they are required to write relevant quotes for all five stories).

Plenary

Gather the class together again. Go through the quotes, checking that all the children have identified the stories correctly. Ask some of the children to read out loud one of the quotes they have made up. Write their quotes on the board and discuss who said them and where the quotation marks should go.

Fairy tale beginnings

1 Once upon a time a little girl lived on the edge of a forest. Her father was a woodcutter and chopped down trees with his huge axe. Her mother said to her one day, "Take this basket of food to Grandmother. It will cheer her up, but be careful when going through the forest."

2 There once lived a little girl with long, golden curls. She lived near a wood. There were bears in the wood.

3 A long time ago, a baby princess was born. The king and queen invited all the good fairies to her christening, but they forgot to ask the evil fairy.

4 In far off times lived a beautiful, kind-hearted girl with two ugly step-sisters and a cruel step-mother who were invited to a ball at the palace.

5 This story took place long ago when all toys were made of wood. Can you believe that an ordinary wooden log could become a real boy?

© May Stevenson

Which is which?

Name: ....

Read the titles on the books below:

Match each of the fairy tale beginnings on sheet 1a to a title on one of the books.

Write your answers here:

Story	Title
Story 1	_____
Story 2	_____
Story 3	_____
Story 4	_____
Story 5	_____

Who said this?

Name: ....

Which story do you think each of these quotations comes from? Draw lines to match the quotations with the correct stories.

1. "Someone has been sitting in my chair," said Father Bear.

2. "You must be back at midnight," said the fairy godmother.

3. "I cannot stop the evil fairy's magic from working, but I can stop the princess from dying," said the good fairy.

4. The fairy explained, "Every time you tell a lie, your nose will grow longer."

5. "All the better to eat you with," grinned the wolf.

Pinocchio

Sleeping Beauty

Little Red Riding Hood

Goldilocks ~ and the Three Bears

Cinderella

Choose one of the fairy tales. Think of two other things people in the story might have said. Write them here. Don't forget to use speech marks.

1. _____

_____

2. _____

_____

Who said this?

Name: ....

Which story do you think each of these quotations comes from?
Write your answers after each quotation.

"Someone has been sitting in my chair,"
said Father Bear.
_____

"You must be back at midnight," said
the fairy godmother.
_____

"I cannot stop the evil fairy's magic from
working, but I can stop the princess
from dying," said the good fairy.
_____

The fairy explained, "Every time you
tell a lie, your nose will grow longer."_____

"All the better to eat you with," grinned
the wolf.
_____

Think of something another character might say in each of the fairy
tales. (It could be in response to the quotations above.) Don't forget to
include speech marks.

1. _____

2. _____

3. _____

4. _____

5. _____

Extension activity
Find some more fairy tales from your class library. Which story has the best
beginning? Why?

2. Moon shadows

Aim

The children will listen to a poem and read it for themselves to gain experience of poetry as a genre. In groups, the children will look at adjectives and similes, and think of alternative words. They will discuss which words or phrases are scary, and which words they like or dislike. More able children will look for examples of alliteration and rhyme.

Activities

Read the poem to the class then give the children sheet **2a** and ask them to read it again for themselves.

Ask the children, in groups, to make a list of scary words from the poem. Ask them to read verse one again to themselves. Can they think about any other images for "curl like ..." and "leap like a ..."?

Distribute copies of sheet **2b** to each group and ask them to work together to answer the questions. Less able children should try to complete the first five. More able children should try to complete Section B as well.

More able children might be asked to write a short poem about shadows, using the words and phrases they have collected.

Plenary

The children should read the poem out loud again in unison as a class. Then each group should reveal the words or phrases which were popular or unpopular with them and give reasons for their choice.

The children should vote as to whether they liked the poem or not, and then whether it felt real or not.

Volunteers may read their own shadow poems if they wish.

Extension activity

Explore shape poems. Show the children some examples, then ask them to write a poem in the shape of a shadow. Mount poems on grey shadow-shaped paper. Make a class book.

Moon shadows

Bright days in summer, and shadows are fun.
Pictures I make with the help of the sun.
I can curl like a hedgehog or leap like a flame.
Whatever the shape, my shadow's the same.

Why, then, in moonlight are shadows so grim?
Spidery, spiky, or wafery thin?
They creep up the curtains and over my bed.
"I'm scared!" cries a worried, wee voice in my head.

Are lizards or snakes or great, giant apes,
Monsters or skeletons making these shapes?
They're not made of nothing – there's something out there.
I'd love to find out, but I really don't dare.

At last morning comes and moonlight is gone.
Shadows have faded with breaking of dawn.
My curtains and bed now look quite all right,
But I cannot forget the fears of the night.

I search for an answer. What made the shapes?
Lampshades? Some pencils? A pile of old tapes?
I cannot be sure, but one thing I know:
Sun shadows are fun, moon shadows are **Oh-h-h-h!**

May Stevenson

Moon shadows

Name: ....

Section A

1. Read the poem with a different person reading each verse.

2. Read verse one again. What other images can you think of using "curl like a …" and "leap like a …"? Make a note of all your suggestions.

3. Read verses two and three again. Think of other words you might use to describe the shapes of shadows in your room at night. Make a note of them all.

4. Make a list of any words in the poem that you a) liked, b) disliked. Why did you like or dislike them?

5. In verse two "spidery" is used. Which word in the next line adds to the effect of making the verse more scary?

Section B

1. Look at verse three. Would you dare to investigate if you thought the shadows might be caused by the things the poet mentions? Why?

2. Look at line eight. Can you think why the worried voice in the poet's head was just a "… wee voice in my head"? ("Wee" is Scottish for "little".) Discuss this in your group.

3. Look through the poem for sets of words in any line which begin with the same sound, such as "can curl" or "leap like". Write them down. Underline the rhyming words at the ends of lines.

4. Using all the words and phrases you have collected, try to write a short poem about shadows. You may use rhyming if you wish, but you do not have to.

3. Heroes don't cry

Aim

The pupils will read an extract from a story and be able to point out words which describe the setting and characters. They will be able to tell (by the use of speech marks) when someone is speaking. They will note that every time someone speaks in a story a new paragraph is taken. They will be able to identify which parts of the speech are statements, questions and exclamations.

Activities

Give each child a copy of sheet **3a** or display it on an overhead projector or interactive computer screen for the class to look at. Give the children time to read the passage for themselves. Discuss with the children which words and phrases suggest to us that the house is empty and has been for some time. If you are using interactive IT a child could circle the correct words.

Discuss what the man looks like and what we learn about him as a character. Why do the children think that he chases Robert and Marie?

Distribute sheet **3b** to the less able children and sheet **3c** to the more able to complete on their own.

Plenary

Bring the children together. Discuss answers to the worksheets.

Extension activity

In the next session show the children a short playscript. Ask them to put "Heroes don't cry" into a playscript format. Have fun acting out the scene.

Heroes don't cry

They raced through a tangled, overgrown shrubbery up to the back of the tall house. Marie hammered on the door while Robert leaned hard on the bell and then banged on a window.

Nobody came. They turned and saw a scowling, bearded face peering over the crumbling wall. He looked evil.

"There's two kids," he shouted. "I'm gonna get them."

"Run!" screamed Robert and grabbed Marie's hand, pulling her behind him.

"We've got to get help," gasped Marie. "What if they catch us?"

Extract by May Stevenson

Heroes don't cry

Name: ....

1. What two things do the children do which first tell us that they are
    desperate for help? Write your answer below.

a)

b)

2. How does the author let us know when someone is speaking in the
    extract?

3. There are several words spoken by characters in the story. Write down
    those which make a question or an order.

a) a question:

b) an order:

Heroes don't cry

Name: ....

1. What three things do the children do which first tell us that they are desperate for help?

a)

b)

c)

2. Underline all the adjectives (describing words) in the extract.

3. There are several words spoken by characters in the extract. Write down those which form a question, an order or a statement.

Tip: Don't forget to use speech marks, question marks or exclamation marks!

a) a question:

b) an order:

c) a statement:

4. On the back of this sheet write at least three more questions of your own. Perhaps an adult is asking you to do something, or you want to buy something from a shopkeeper.

4. Themes in fairy tales

Aim

The children will read and refer to several fairy tales and understand the various themes running through them. They will be aware of the difference in style between traditional fairy tales and modern stories.

Activities

A good selection of fairy stories will be needed, for example, Cinderella, Jack and the Beanstalk, Aladdin, etc.

Discuss the word "theme" with the children. If they have been to a theme park they may want to talk about it. Point out that the theme of a story is what it is all about, for instance, it may be a good person defeating an evil one.

Divide the class into small, mixed ability groups and ask them to think of fairy tales that would fit each of the themes given on sheet **4a**. Have the fairy stories available for them to look at. Examples of possible answers might be:

> Good defeating evil – Cinderella
> A weak character defeating a strong one – Jack and the Beanstalk
> A truthful person defeating someone who tells lies – Aladdin

After ten minutes gather the children together and discuss their answers. Give the less able children sheet **4b** to fill in. Hand out sheet **4c** to the other children and ask them to fill in any other fairy stories they can think of. They will need to search through books.

Plenary

Ask the children if the fairy stories they have been working with are similar to stories in modern children's books. Ask for differences or similarities. Read out a few examples of the beginnings of fairy tales and modern stories, and compare them as a class. Ask why the pupils think fairy stories were told to children.

Extension activity

Some children may want to write a short fairy story of their own.

Story themes

Good defeating evil.

A wise person defeating a foolish one.

A weak character defeating a strong one.

Someone who has to battle against great difficulties, winning in the end.

A truthful person defeating someone who tells lies.

Themes in fairy tales

Name: ....

Once upon a time there was an ugly duckling who was laughed at and chased away by the other ducks because he was different. Then he grew into a swan and became stronger and more beautiful than the ducks, and he was very happy.

What is the theme in this story?

_____

_____

Many years ago some animals were having a contest. A large hare was picked to race against a tortoise. The hare laughed at the idea of the tortoise beating him. He ran off laughing and then decided he had lots of time and laid down to have a sleep. The little tortoise kept plodding on and eventually passed the sleeping hare, and went on to win the contest.

What is the theme in this story?

_____

_____

Name: ....

Title	Story beginning	Story ending	Theme

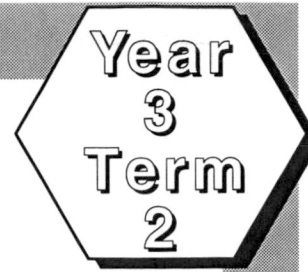

5. Story beginnings and endings

Aim

The children will read the beginnings and endings of some traditional stories, looking at and discussing the traditional language in them. They will then use similar language in writing the opening to a fairy tale of their own.

Activities

Divide the children into several mixed ability groups. Distribute sheet **5a** to half of the class and sheet **5b** to the other half. Let them discuss the sheets and determine from which traditional story the lines come. Discuss the use of traditional language. Which words or phrases make it sound old?

Ask children from group **5a** to read aloud the story beginnings on their sheet, and ask the children in group **5b** to say if they match the endings they have.

Establish which story beginning matches which ending and either read them aloud or write them on the board.

Next, write the title "The Evil Wizard and the Frog" on the board. Ask the children to write the opening to a story. More able children could write an ending as well.

Plenary

Ask the children to compare their writing with the openings of some of the books they have read. Point out that in the past not everyone was able to read, and so it was important to have familiar beginnings and endings in stories to make it easier for people to follow them when they were being told.

Story beginnings

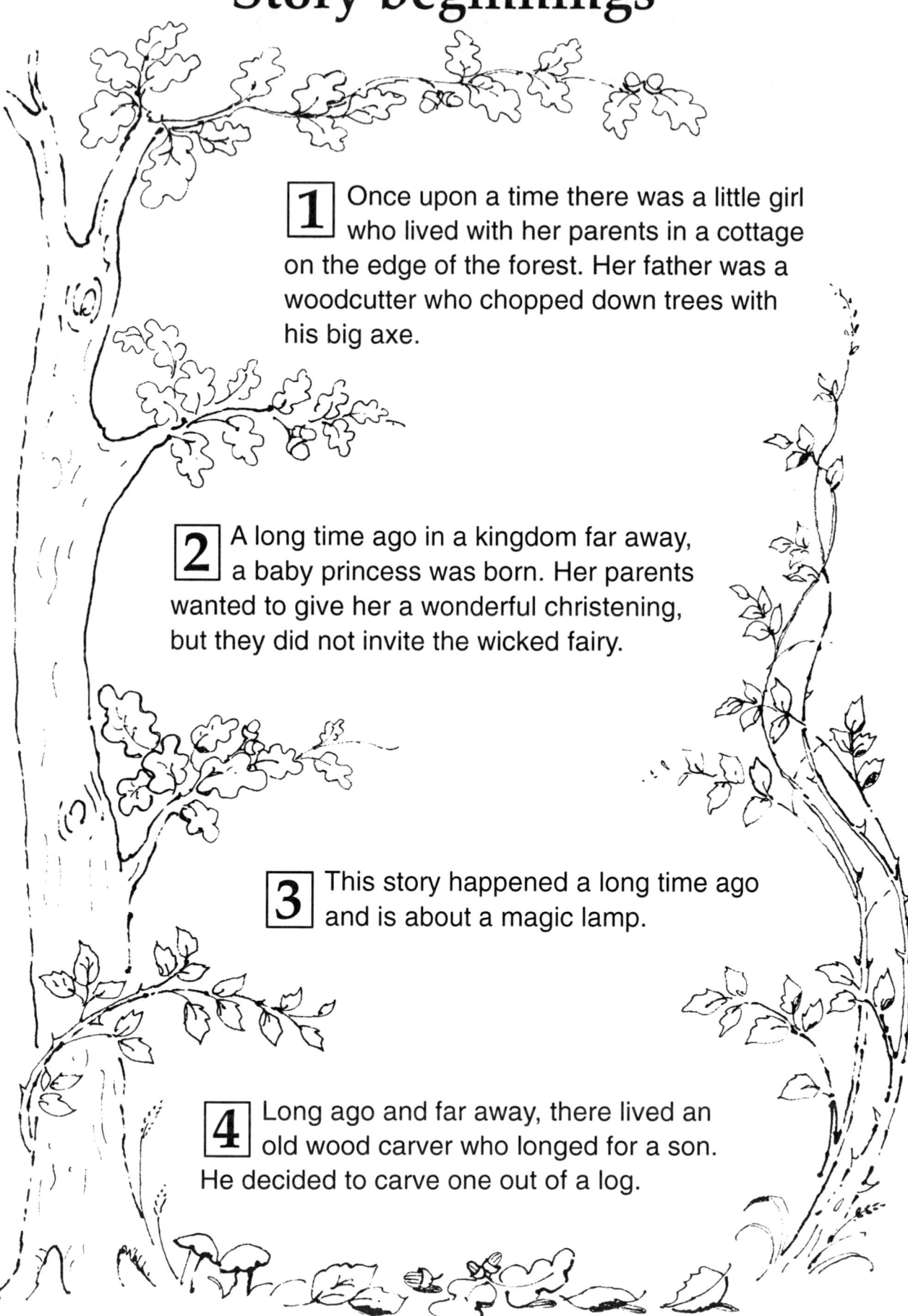

1 Once upon a time there was a little girl who lived with her parents in a cottage on the edge of the forest. Her father was a woodcutter who chopped down trees with his big axe.

2 A long time ago in a kingdom far away, a baby princess was born. Her parents wanted to give her a wonderful christening, but they did not invite the wicked fairy.

3 This story happened a long time ago and is about a magic lamp.

4 Long ago and far away, there lived an old wood carver who longed for a son. He decided to carve one out of a log.

Story endings

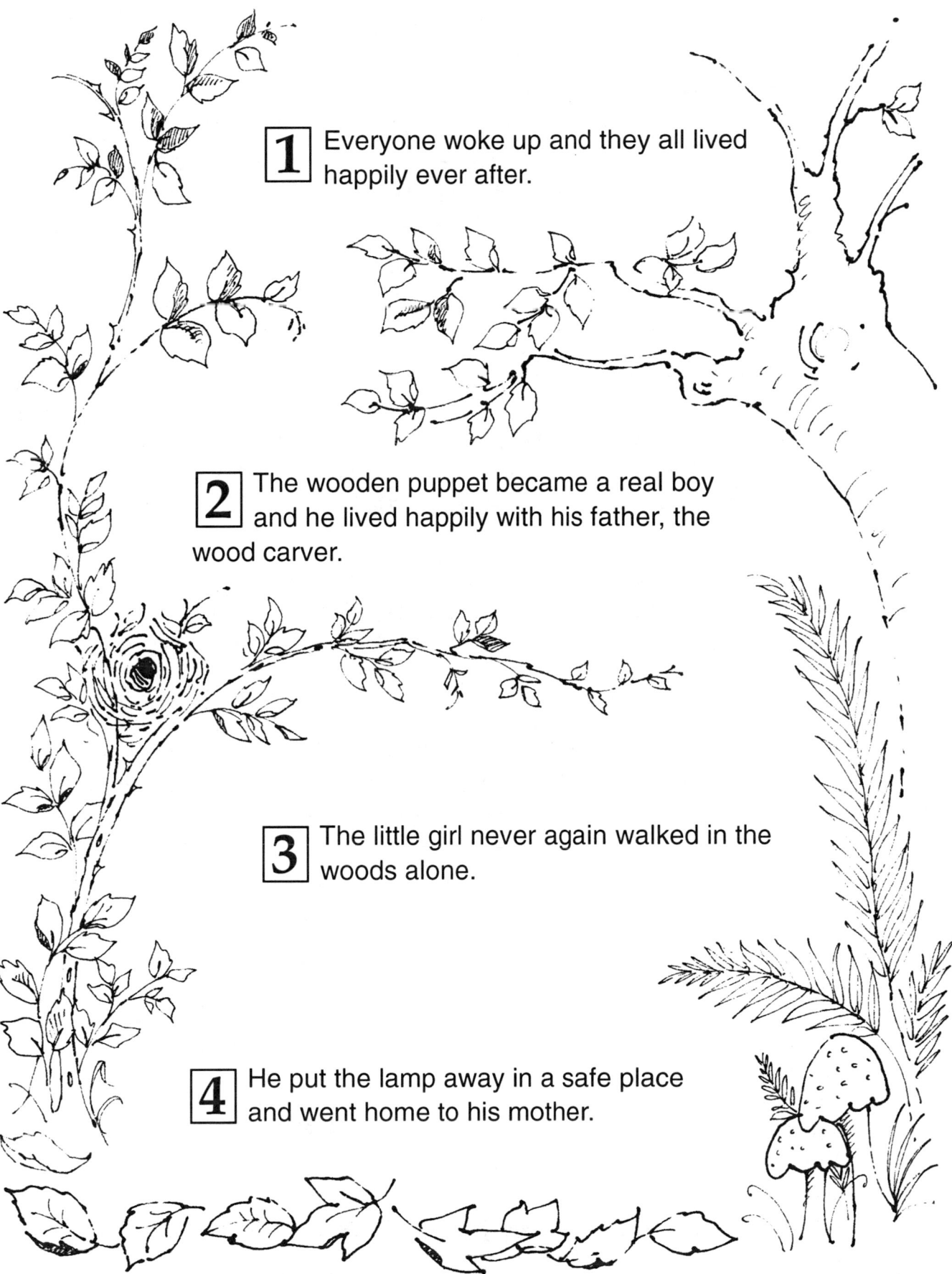

1 Everyone woke up and they all lived happily ever after.

2 The wooden puppet became a real boy and he lived happily with his father, the wood carver.

3 The little girl never again walked in the woods alone.

4 He put the lamp away in a safe place and went home to his mother.

Brilliant Activities for Reading Fiction

6. Character study

Aim

The children will focus their learning on the "bad" characters in a poetry text and in the fairy tales used in the last two chapters. They will look at the features of a poem and, using the poem as a stimulus for reading and writing skills, they will create their own "bad" character, and plan and write a poem about her.

Activities

Ask the children to think back to the fairy stories you have shared recently. Get them to think about the characters in the stories.

What is a character? Who are the good and bad characters? List the bad ones on a board, then ask the children why they think fairy tales always have a "baddie". Does the evil character ever win? Why?

Read the poetry text on sheet **6a** together, using separate copies or an interactive computer screen. Discuss the descriptive language. Which words or phrases make the character bad? Does he/she do anything bad? Does the character win or lose in the end?

Ask the children to look at the layout. Get them to realize it is a poem. Look at how each line begins with a capital letter. What punctuation marks are there? Does the poem rhyme or not? Does poetry have to rhyme?

Explain to the children that they are all going to write a short poem about a witch. They need to make her "bad"; she looks bad, she does bad things and she loses in the end. Ask for some ideas in the discussion group. Brainstorm ideas on the board. Give each child a copy of the planning sheet **6b** and give them ten minutes to jot their ideas down. Then they may start their poems.

Plenary

Bring everyone together to read volunteers' poems. Discuss.

Extension activity

Re-draft the poems to make a display or class book, or get groups to act out their favourites.

The monster

The monster is an ugly, hideous sight
With glaring eyes, he's a terrifying fright,

He has no friends and lives alone
In a dark, damp cave, chewing on bones,

He grunts, he snarls, he shouts and yells,
He never washes, he burps, and he SMELLS!

He's going out to look for his lunch,
A child to kill? More bones to munch,

But filled with all his evil thoughts,
His nasty, old brain is out of sorts,

For he doesn't notice a rock, you see,
So trips and falls and … oh yippee!

Down he plunges into the ocean below,
Now he'll never come back, and so …

The children are safe from that horrible beast,
Never again on their bones will he feast!

Paula Goodridge

The witch

Name: ....

Think of words to describe your witch and write them around the hat:

What does she do that is bad?

What happens to her at the end?

Draw a picture of your witch in the box below:

7. Jenny on the ginger jar

Aim

Children will read an extract from a story, noting how the opening affects the reader and how tension is built up through the use of adjectives. They will then discuss and write about what they think the character might feel and why.

Activities

Read the text on sheet **7a** to the children and then ask some children to read it aloud again. Ask what they think might be happening in the story. Ask them to look for adjectives that make it seem scary. Would a beginning like this make them want to read more of the story? Listen to as many opinions as possible.

Ask what they think Beth would feel and what she might do next. Ask what they would do if it happened to them.

Ask the less able children to complete sheet **7b** and give them help where necessary.

Ask the more able children to complete sheet **7c**.

Plenary

Bring the class together again. Read the questions on sheet **7c** and have children from that group answer them. Then do the same with sheet **7b**. Read the extract again and ask for general opinions about the story beginning and what might follow. Ask to hear their ideas about what might happen next.

Extension activity

Revise alliteration. Ask children to add words to the text to make alliteration.

Read poems with examples of alliteration. Ask children to make up their own sentences showing alliteration.

Jenny on the ginger jar

Beth looked up and rubbed her eyes. Surely she must be imagining this? But round the bottom of her bed a mist, cold and hazy, swirled and twirled. Soft, frothy-grey fronds danced back and forth as they curled towards the low ceiling of the attic. Then, from the darkest corner of the room, where the nightlight threw deep shadows, a small voice whispered, "Beth, Beth."

Extract by May Stevenson

Jenny on the ginger jar

Name: ....

1. Find two words which describe the mist.

a)

b)

2. Find two words which tell us how the mist moved.

a)

b)

3. In which room is this story taking place? (Circle the correct answer.)

a) the kitchen   b) the garden   c) the attic

4. Pretend you are Beth. Write what is happening and how you are feeling.

Jenny on the ginger jar

Name: ....

Answer these questions in sentences:

1. Why did Beth rub her eyes?

2. What might have made the frothy-grey fronds? Look up the word 'frond' in your dictionary to help you.

3. Where in the house did this take place?

4. Where did the voice come from?

5. Who do you think called Beth's name?

6. What do you think Beth will do or say next?

7. Pretend you are Beth and write in your own words, what you feel and what you will do next. Use the back of the sheet if you need to.

8. Vek's visit

Aim

The children will read an extract from a story and discuss its genre. They will consider how the characters in the story might feel and react, and discuss what might happen next. They will look at humour in the story and discuss metaphorical phrases.

Activities

Read the extract on sheet **8a** to the children and ask what kind of story they think it is (science fiction). What tells us this? Who or what do they think Vek is? How do they think Miss Rolie feels with such a strange boy in her class? How do they think the children will react? How would they feel if it happened in their class? What do they think will happen next?

Distribute sheet **8a** and ask four children to read a paragraph each. Ask the children if they enjoyed the extract. Did they find it funny? Why?

Divide the class into two groups. Ask the less able children to complete as much as possible of sheet **8b**, giving help where needed. Ask the more able group to complete sheets **8b** and **8c**.

Plenary

Bring the children together again and take answers orally for all the questions on sheet **8b**. Discuss where necessary.

Ask the questions on sheet **8c** orally, giving the less able children the chance to join in if they wish. Make a list on the blackboard of funny or odd things people say when they mean something else.

Ask several children to tell this story in their own words.

Vek's visit

"Jump to it!" Miss Rolie cried. "Last thing for to-day, I want you to run round the room as fast as you can. Zip your mouth tightly shut, step on it and keep your eyes peeled for each other."

Vek took an enormous jump and landed underneath the gym teacher's face. He smiled up at her. Then his fingers felt around his lips. He turned to Jamie and whispered, "What is a zip? Is it the same as a lip?"

Before Jamie could reply, Vek was reaching up to remove an eye,

so that he could peel it. Just then all the lights in the gym went out. It was very dark for a moment then a humming sound could be heard and the room was lit by a soft glow.

"It is time, Jamie," Vek called. "My ship has arrived. I must scatter some forgetful dust before I go. Thank you for everything I have learned and goodbye."

Extract by May Stevenson

Vek's visit

Name: ....

1. Which words tell us that the children were not in their classroom?

2. Was Jamie of any use to Vek? How do you know?

3. What was Vek about to do which tells us he is not human?

4. Who or what do you think Vek might be?

5. What kind of ship do you think has arrived?

6. Describe the planet that Vek may have come from.

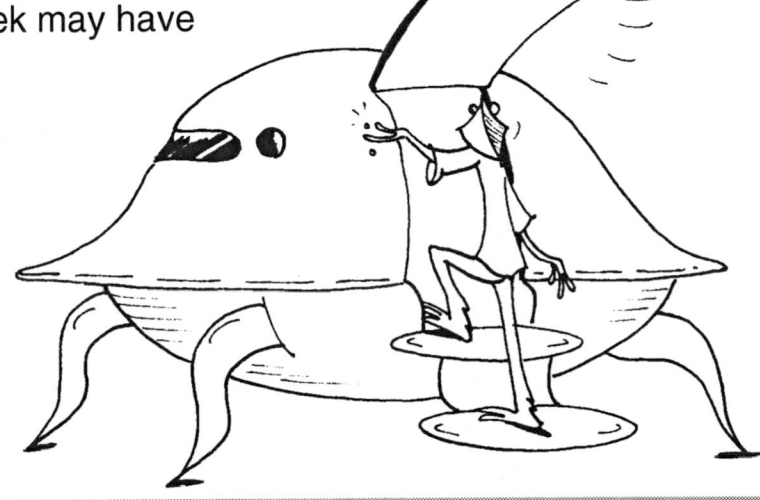

Vek's visit

Name: ....

1. What exactly do you think Miss Rolie meant by:

a) "jump to it"

b) "zip your mouth tightly shut"

c) "step on it"

d) "keep your eyes peeled"

2. Make a list of any other funny or odd things that people say when they mean something else, for example, "You'd better pull your socks up." Compare your list with a friend's.

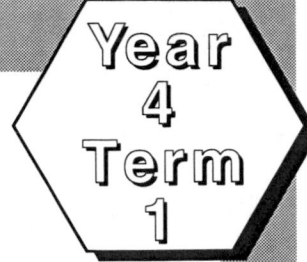

9. Vek goes to school

Aim

The children will read an extract from a story and look at how the author creates recognizable characters and allows the reader to understand how they are thinking and feeling by their actions and speech. They will take the two main characters in this extract, and discuss the differences between them and how they react to the same circumstances. Children will then discuss popular authors and why they like them.

Activities

Read the text on sheet **9a** to the class. Divide the class into two groups according to ability. The more able children should tackle as many as possible of the questions on sheet **9c**.

Read the text to the less able children again, asking one or two of them to read bits out loud. The children should then try to answer the questions on sheet **9b**. Give them help where needed.

Plenary

Bring the children together again and go through the sheet discussing answers. Take as many views as possible about how the children would feel if this happened in their classroom. Hear the accounts of the teacher's point of view. Discuss how Miss Wode and Vek are two very different characters and the difference between their reactions to what is happening.

Discuss the types of books the children like, and ask if they can name their favourite authors and say why they like their books.

Vek goes to school

Miss Wode grew very pink in the face and shouted more loudly, "I want your eyes on the board immediately!" Vek obeyed. He unscrewed one of his eyes and placed it in the middle of the taking away sum that Miss Wode had prepared. The teacher's face grew redder and she clung to the edge of her table.

"Put your heads on your arms this minute," she squealed.

Then, as Jamie sat looking down at his feet, he had a horrible thought. What if Vek took off his head and laid it on his arms? Miss Wode might die of fright. Slowly he lifted his eyes and glanced at his friend. He was sitting with a puzzled look on his face. Then slowly he put both hands up to his neck and felt all around it. Then he began to twist and turn his head.

"Please Miss Wode, I feel dizzy," Jamie called out. "Can I sit up?"

"Dizzy? Why are you dizzy? Didn't you have any breakfast?" She didn't wait for an answer.

"Go and get your milk," she said. "Come to think of it, you can all have your milk." Then still thinking that Vek might be the headmaster's nephew, she forced a half smile and asked, "Would you like a bottle? Then you can all have a break," she added.

"Thank you," Vek said. First he rescued his eye from the blackboard. Then he flicked the foil top off a bottle, poured the milk out of the window, broke the bottle and crunched up the glass.

"Nice," he commented. Miss Wode fled from the room.

Extract by May Stevenson

128 − 33 =

Vek goes to school

Name: ....

1. What was the first sign that Miss Wode was upset?

2. Why do you think she clung to the edge of the table?

3. What did Jamie think might happen if Vek removed his head?

4. What did Jamie do to draw Miss Wode's attention away from Vek?

5. Why was Miss Wode trying hard to be nice to this strange pupil?

6. How would you feel if this happened in your classroom?

128 – 33 =

Vek goes to school

Name: ....

1. What was the first sign that Miss Wode was upset?

2. Why do you think she clung to the edge of the table?

3. What did Jamie think might happen if Vek removed his head?

4. What did Jamie do to draw Miss Wode's attention away from Vek?

5. Why was Miss Wode trying hard to be nice to this strange pupil?

6. How would you feel if this happened in your classroom?

7. What kind of books do you like? Humorous? Science fiction? Mystery? Magic? Supernatural? Adventure? Historic? School stories? Sport?

8. Who is your favourite author and why?

$128 - 33 =$

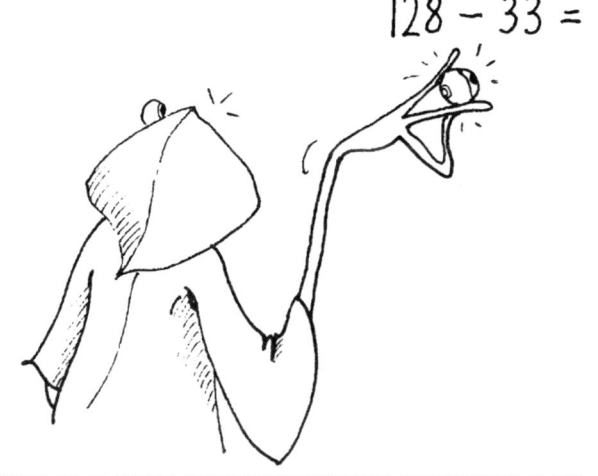

9. The class would probably be amused by Vek's antics but Miss Wode might see things very differently. Write a short account of this scene from the teacher's point of view.

10. Character descriptions

Aim

The children will read extracts from two stories written in the nineteenth century and note archaic language. From the character descriptions, they will see how the authors use words to build up recognizable characters. They will be able to form an opinion about the characters. This will also encourage an interest in classic stories.

Activities

Give the children copies of sheets **10a** and **10b**, or display the texts from them on an overhead projector or interactive computer screen for the class to look at.

Read aloud the extract by Louisa May Alcott on sheet **10a** and discuss all the difficult or old-fashioned words with the children. Do the same with the extract by Charles Dickens on sheet **10b**. Explain to the children that in the time when these were written, books were one of the few forms of entertainment available, and so people liked them to last a long time and be full of description. There were also few, if any, pictures in the books and so the author had to describe things at great length for the reader. Children of these times had no radio or television and few toys to amuse them and they depended on books to pass the time.

Give the less able children sheet **10a** and go over it with them before asking them to answer the questions.

Hand out sheet **10b** to the more able children and ask them to complete the questions.

Plenary

Bring the groups together again. Check the answers to the questions from both groups. Ask the children to describe one of the characters in their own words. Would they like to meet them? Why?

Extension activity

The children could be asked to give a description of a character from a classic story that they have read about or perhaps seen on screen.

Character descriptions

Name: ....

Fifteen-year-old Jo was very tall, thin and brown, and reminded one of a colt, for she never seemed to know what to do with her long limbs, which were very much in her way. She had a decided mouth, a comical nose, and sharp, grey eyes, which appeared to see everything, and were by turns fierce, funny or thoughtful.

from Little Women *by Louisa May Alcott (1832–1888)*

---

1. What age was Jo?

2. Was Jo a small girl? Which words tell us?

3. What did Jo remind the author of? What is this animal?

4. What colour were Jo's eyes?

5. What was her nose like?

Character descriptions

Name: ....

> Scrooge! A squeezing, wrenching, grasping, scraping,
> clutching, covetous, old sinner! The cold within him froze his
> old features, nipped his pointed nose, shrivelled his cheek,
> stiffened his gait, made his eyes red, his thin lips blue.
>
> *from* A Christmas Carol *by Charles Dickens (1812–1870)*

1. Scrooge was a "miser". Look up the word "miser" in a dictionary. What does it mean?

2. Does the name "Scrooge" suit him? Why?

3. What does "covetous" mean?

4. What is a "sinner"?

5. What does the author mean by "the cold within him"? Have a guess.

6. Why do you think Scrooge was "grasping"?

7. What does "his gait" mean?

8. Do you think Scrooge was a nice or nasty character? How do we know this from the text?

11. The whole truth

Aim

The children will read and perform a play script. They will understand how a play script differs from a story in layout, noting the character list, scene, stage directions and characters' lines. They will read the script with a view to deciding what happens next.

Activities

Each child should be given a copy of the script on sheets **11a** and **11b**. A narrator and three characters should be chosen and the play read through from the beginning to the end of the piece. The narrator reads the stage directions, which are in italics.

Divide the children into groups of four of mixed ability. Ask them to choose the three characters and the narrator and read the play through. Do the same again, changing the characters around.

Bring the class together again, issue sheet **11c** and ask all of the children to try to complete it. Give help where needed to less able children.

Plenary

Bring the class together again and discuss the answers to the questions. Ask for individual opinions as to how the play might end.

Extension activity

You could give the children the chance to write an ending for the play (in the correct form) and let them act it out.

The whole truth

Characters:

Mother: a housewife

Becky: her daughter

Simon: her nephew

SCENE 1: IN THE GARDEN

Becky and Simon are sitting quite far apart on the grass. Becky looks very unhappy. Mother enters.

Mother: Hello, you two. Having fun?

Simon: Yes, thank you, Aunt Mary.

Becky runs into the house and Mother looks surprised.

Simon: It's all right, Aunt Mary. I think Becky needs to go to the toilet.

Mother: It's not like Becky to run away so rudely.

Simon: Shall I go and fetch her?

Mother: No thank you, dear. Your Mum will be here at any minute.

Mother goes into the house but cannot find Becky. She comes back looking worried.

The whole truth (continued)

Mother: Simon, where can she have gone?

Simon: Well, she did say that she was hiding something from you, Aunt Mary. I don't like to tell tales, but I think she's been stealing.

Mother: What?

Simon: Yes. Some money and jewellery.

Becky appears at the back door. She has a bundle of notes and some necklaces in her hands. Simon jumps up.

Simon: See! I told you, Aunt Mary.

Becky: Honestly Mum, I haven't stolen anything. He must have done it and put them in my bedroom. I've just found them. He punched me too. Look!

She points to a bruise on her leg.

Mother: Oh, Becky. How could you? And to try to blame it on your cousin!

The whole truth

Name: ....

1. In a play, how do we know when the setting for a scene is being described?

2. Where does it tell us who is going to appear in the play?

3. How do we know when each person is supposed to speak?

4. How do we know right at the beginning that the two children are not happy?

5. Who do you think is guilty of stealing?

6. How do you think it might end?

12. The lamplighter

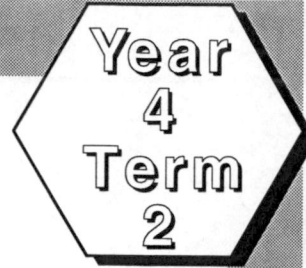

Aim

The children will read a nineteenth-century poem and recognize archaic words. Unfamiliar words will be listed and their meanings explained. The children will identify and understand expressive language which describes moods and emotions. They will also take note of rhyming couplets.

Activities

Explain what a lamplighter used to do. Hand out sheet **12a** to the whole class. Read verse one to the children and then have a child read it again. Ask the children if there are any words they don't understand and put their meanings on the board. Read verses two and three and follow the same procedure. Ask the children to identify which words show that the poem was written a long time ago.

Let the children read the poem again. The less able children should complete sheet **12b**. The more able can answer the questions on sheet **12c**.

Plenary

Bring the children together again and discuss their answers. Discuss the loneliness of this child and how they feel about it. How might a child of this era amuse himself for long periods? Ask for words which they might use today if they were ill and lonely. Find out how many children enjoyed the poem.

The lamplighter

My tea is nearly ready and the sun has left the sky,
It's time to take the window to see Leerie going by,
For every night at teatime and before you take your seat,
With lantern and with ladder he comes posting up the street.

Now Tom would be a driver and Maria go to sea,
And my papa's a banker and as rich as he can be,
But I, when I am stronger and can choose what I'm to do,
O Leerie, I'll go round at night and light the lamps with you!

For we are very lucky, with a lamp before the door,
And Leerie stops to light it as he lights so many more,
And O! before you hurry by with ladder and with light,
O Leerie, see a little child and nod to him tonight!

Robert Louis Stevenson (1850 – 1894)

The lamplighter

Name: ....

1. What is Leerie's job?

2. What does the child want to be when he grows up?

3. What job does his father do?

4. What two objects is Leerie carrying?

5. Choose three pairs of rhyming words from the poem:

a)

b)

c)

The lamplighter

Name: ....

1. The poet says "the sun has left the sky". What does he mean?

2. What does he mean by "take the window"?

3. What do you think Leerie is doing when he is "posting up the street"?

4. What tells us that the poet's family was not poor?

5. How do we know that the poet was not very well?

6. Tom and Maria seem to be friends or acquaintances of the poet. What did Tom want to do when he grew up? What did Maria want to do?

7. What does the poet want to do when he grows up?

8. Why do you think he wants to be a lamplighter?

9. If he gets better and grows strong, do you think he will still want to be a lamplighter? Say why.

10. What tells us that the poet is lonely, and that he does not see very many people and is anxious to make friends?

13. The creature in the cave

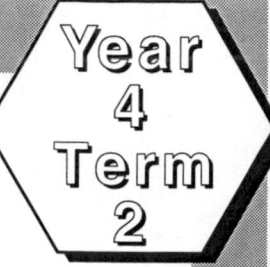

Year
4
Term
2

Aim

The children will read an extract from a modern story and consider the language writers use to create an imaginary setting. They will identify figurative language in the story, such as similes and alliteration, and discuss how these add to the effectiveness of the piece.

Activities

Read the extract from the story to the children then hand out sheet **13a** to everyone. Give the children turns at reading the piece again. Discuss it with them.

Explain what a simile is and ask the children to find an example in the text. Explain what alliteration is and ask the children if they can find an example of this in the text.

Divide the children into two groups. Give sheet **13b** to the less able group. Give out sheet **13c** to the more able and ask them to complete it on their own.

Plenary

Bring the children together again and discuss their answers to the worksheets. Check their answers to the questions about alliteration and similes, and ask them for any more examples that they can think of. Why do they think the writer chose to use these devices in the story? Did they find it easy to picture the scene?

Find out what the children think might actually have happened to Joshan. Did he imagine the whole episode?

The creature in the cave

"That's strange," Joshan said to himself. "I've never seen this cave before."

He climbed over a rock and in his hurry, bumped his head, but simply rubbed the sore bit and went on.

He stepped into the entrance and his eyes grew as wide as saucers. The walls of the cave were decorated with streamers and sparkling stars, and a soft, shimmering glow came from somewhere in the back. Who could have done this?

"Hello," he said in a small voice, feeling as nervous as a kitten.

A shape moved at the back of the cave. Then Joshan saw a strawberry-pink creature which reminded him of an octopus, crawl forwards. Its head was like a giant piece of bubble gum, except for the large mouth on top of it. One tentacle reached out and slithered towards Joshan. It felt the bump on his head, then his face and hair, and his legs and feet. Joshan couldn't move, but the pain in his head was gone.

Suddenly the whole cave was lit with a blinding blue light.

"Forgive me," the creature said. "I am needed. You see, we have many places on Earth to cleanse before we can settle here. Goodbye."

The light disappeared. So did the creature and the streamers and stars. Joshan saw a parcel at the back of the cave. It was marked "to be collected." It was full of cartons, cans, bottles and other disgusting rubbish. But who, or what, would collect it?

Extract by May Stevenson

The creature in the cave

Name: ....

1. What was it like inside the cave?

2. Find these similes in the text and complete them:

a) his eyes grew as _____

b) feeling as nervous as _____

c) Its head was like _____

3. Why do you think the creature came to the cave?

4. Use a pencil to underline any examples of alliteration in the text.

The creature in the cave

Name: ....

1. How does the writer let us know that this is no ordinary cave?

2. Which words describe the movement of the creature?

3. The author has used three similes. Try to find them. (A simile is where an author uses "like" or "as" to describe something.)

4. There are several examples of alliteration in the text. Identify them and write them down. (Alliteration is using the same sound at the beginning of words close to each other).

5. Joshan couldn't move. Why do you think this was?

6. What do you think might happen next?

14. The seasons

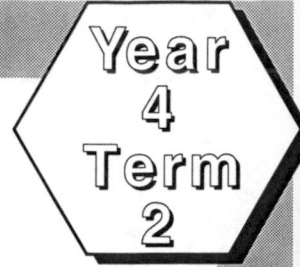

Aim

The children will read a poem, understand the meaning of verse, rhythm, alliteration and rhyme, and be able to identify each of these. They will read and clap out the syllables in each line. They will note how the writer involves the senses in describing things, and consider why the poem may have been written.

Activities

Hand out a copy of sheet **14a** to each child. As a class, give various children the chance to read a verse of the poem aloud and then ask the class to read the verses while clapping the rhythm as they read it. Do this several times until all the children seem to be happy with it.

Hand out sheet **14b** and ask which verses describe summer, winter, autumn and spring (question 1). Ask the children questions 2 and 3 as a class. When the children seem at ease with this, ask them to write answers to all of the questions, giving help where needed to the less able children.

Plenary

Bring the class together again and ask for answers to the questions. Take examples of alliteration and write them on the board.

Ask the children what the poem tells us about the seasons. How useful do they think it would be for teaching children about nature? Why might the poem have been written?

Extension activity

The children could write a verse of poetry of their own about one of the seasons and read this to the class.

The seasons

Meadows of mayflowers, butterflies and bees,
Children whose ice-creams drip on their knees,
Feet on the firm sand, then splash in the sea,
Run back to the sand dune, hungry for tea.

Carpet of bluebells, lambs on the hills,
Birds singing sweetly, new daffodils,
Silky-soft chickens, fluffy to hold,
Warm hot cross buns, to keep out the cold.

Church bells are ringing, stars in the sky,
Ice on the windows, snow is piled high,
Mince pies and fresh cream, Christmas cake too,
Parcels of presents, from me to you.

Squirrels in the trees, leaping around,
Leaves red and yellow, fall to the ground,
Sparks from a bonfire, light up the night,
Sausages sizzle, ready to bite.

Unknown

The seasons

Name: ....

1. Read the four verses and then decide which one describes:

a) spring

b) summer

c) autumn

d) winter

2. Choose one of the verses and find words in it which talk about:

a) seeing

b) hearing

c) smelling

d) tasting

e) touching

3. Write down any examples of alliteration you can find (where the same sound is used at the beginning of words close to each other, for example, "sausages sizzle".)

4. Find pairs of rhyming words.

15. Simple verses

Aim

The children will read simple traditional verses including a proverb, clapping out the rhythm of each line, and in doing so, count the syllables in them. They will be aware of how simple verses might be used to teach something and look for examples of alliteration and rhyme.

Activities

Divide the class into four groups. Hand out sheet **15a** and let each group read a different verse, clapping out each line as they read. Change round so that the children have a chance to read all of the verses out loud.

Ask if they can see why parents would teach such verses to children (for counting, remembering months of the year or days of the week, etc.). Ask the children to spot alliteration in any of the lines. Ask them to find rhyming words in any of the verses. Talk about these. Discuss the fourth poem, and ask whether they think this is true or not and for reasons why. Explain that this verse is a proverb as it has a moral and gives advice about something. Can the children think of any other proverbs?

Hand out sheet **15b** to the less able children and sheet **15c** to the more able, and ask them to complete them.

Plenary

Gather the children together and take oral answers to each question, checking that they all understand the correct answers. Let the children recite any simple verses that they have been taught and think of why they were taught them.

Simple verses

1
One, two – buckle my shoe,
Three, four – open the door,
Five, six – pick up sticks,
Seven, eight – lay them straight,
Nine, ten – a big fat hen,
Eleven, twelve – I hope you're well,
Thirteen, fourteen – draw the curtain,
Fifteen, sixteen – the maid's in the kitchen,
Seventeen, eighteen – she's in waiting,
Nineteen, twenty – my stomach's empty.

2
Thirty days hath September,
April, June and November,
All the rest have thirty-one,
Except for February alone,
Which has twenty-eight days clear,
And twenty-nine in each leap year.

3
If you sneeze on a Monday, you sneeze for danger,
Sneeze on a Tuesday, kiss a stranger,
Sneeze on a Wednesday, sneeze for a letter,
Sneeze on a Thursday, something better,
Sneeze on a Friday, sneeze for sorrow,
Sneeze on a Saturday, joy tomorrow.

4
Early to bed and early to rise,
Makes a man healthy, wealthy and wise.

Simple verses

Name: ....

Make a list of all the rhyming words you can find in the verses:

eg. _____two_____ _____shoe_____

_____ _____

_____ _____

_____ _____

_____ _____

_____ _____

_____ _____

_____ _____

_____ _____

_____ _____

_____ _____

_____ _____

_____ _____

_____ _____

_____ _____

_____ _____

Simple verses

Name: ....

1. Find two examples of alliteration in the verses. (Alliteration is using the same sound at the beginning of words close to each other.) Write them down.

2. Circle the rhyming words in each verse.

3. What might you use each verse for?

4. Does the last verse tell the truth? Why? Which bits of it do you think are true, and why?

Read the following traditional verse and answer the questions:

> Bow, wow, wow!
> Whose dog art thou?
> Little Tommy Tinker's dog,
> Bow, wow, wow!

5. What tells you that this is an old verse?

6. Write down the words where alliteration is used.

7. How might a mother use this verse with her child?

8. Try to think of a simple nursery rhyme that you learned as a child and tell it to your group.

16. New neighbours

Aim

The aim of this text is to raise the children's awareness of another culture, and to discuss the social and emotional issues raised. The children will also look at how paragraphs are used in writing.

Activities

Hand out sheet **16a** and read the text with the children. Discuss the content and ask questions about it. Why did the family come to England? How might they feel? How does the speaker react to them? How can cultures vary?

Ask the children to identify the paragraphs. Why do writers use paragraphs?

The less able children will have questions to answer on sheet **16b**. To vary interest, you could cut up the questions into strips, put them in envelopes, give each pair of children an envelope and get them to answer the questions orally. Discuss the questions with them.

Explain to the more able children that they are going to pretend to be Anna. They will write an account of her move to England using paragraphs. Give them sheet **16c**.

Plenary

Bring the children together as a class. Ask the less able children to pick a question from their envelope to test the more able. This will give them a great confidence boost and is fun for the more able too! Discuss answers. Ask volunteers from the more able to read their accounts of Anna's arrival. Discuss.

Extension activity

Use information books, atlases or the internet to find out more facts about Poland.

New neighbours

(Dedicated to Gabriel, Edyta, Aleks and Piotr)

A family moved into the flat next door just before Easter. Mum and I went to see them to welcome them into the neighbourhood. We found out that they are Polish. The father, Piotr, or Peter as it's usually spelt in English, speaks good English and he explained that he came to England six months ago because he could get a better job here. There is a lot of unemployment in Poland and the jobs that people can get are poorly paid. He has just brought his family over to be with him.

Peter's wife, Anna, is very beautiful and she smiles a lot, but she doesn't speak any English. They have a son called Pawel, who is almost two years old and a son called Gabriel, who is ten like me. He will come to my school. He speaks a bit of English. It must be very hard for Anna not to understand anything. How will she go shopping or make friends, I wonder?

Gabriel started school, but I think he felt very lost. I played football with him at playtime. He liked that. He couldn't understand our teacher at first but we all help him. I think he will learn to speak English quite quickly. He is a nice boy. Mum bought a Polish dictionary so she could talk to Anna when Peter is at work all day. Anna misses her friends and family in Poland. I looked in my atlas today to find out where Poland is in Europe. I have learned "hello" in Polish but it seems like a hard language to learn. I do not understand a word when the family talk together. I think I will go to the library to find books about Poland.

Anna invited me for tea today. We had food which I had not tasted before. Peter told me it was pickled red cabbage and pork and some kind of dumpling they make in Poland. It was delicious. They are very kind. Anna is lovely. Even though we cannot speak each other's language we like each other. I smile at her and she smiles back.

Mum asked Peter if they celebrated Easter like we do. He said they go to church and have a special dinner. They make boiled eggs and eat them with horseradish sauce. They do not have any chocolate eggs so I think I will save my pocket money and buy one for Gabriel and Pawel. I like my new neighbours very much.

Paula Goodridge

New neighbours

Name: ....

1. Why did the Polish family come to England?

2. Who speaks the best English?

3. How do you think Gabriel felt in an English school?

4. Why does the writer like the family?

5. Do you think the writer wants to learn more about Poland? Why?

6. What is different about the way the Polish celebrate Easter?

7. How do you think Anna feels to be in England?

New neighbours

Name: ....

Pretend you are Anna. Write an account of your move to England. How do you feel? What is different for you and your children? (Try to write using paragraphs.)

17. Reading reviews

Aim

The aim of this chapter is to get the children to think about which books they read themselves and to think about different genres of reading and writing materials. This is a good end of term activity, as they can reflect on what they have read recently, giving you the chance to reinforce their learning.

Activities

Ask the children to tell you as many different types of books as they can (such as stories, plays, poetry, atlases, etc.). Write a list on the board. Explain that you would like them to think about their favourite "genres". Give sheet **17a** to the less able children and ask them to fill it in.

The more able readers will be working in groups of about four to six. They are going to investigate what reading material is in their classroom. Choose a team leader from each group and give them sheet **17b**.

Plenary

Bring the children together again and ask for volunteers to read their answers. Discuss any views which the children have about improving the availability of reading materials in the classroom.

Extension activity

Make a collaborative wall display about reading. Get the children to design what goes on it. Evaluate the results with them.

What do you read?

Name: ....

1. What do you like to read (put a circle around your favourites)?

    poems   picture books   plays

       stories with no pictures   atlases

    information books   diaries   comics

2. What book are you reading now?

    Title: _____

    Author: _____

3. What is it about?

4. If you could buy some books for your classrom what kind of books would you buy? Why?

Classroom detectives

Name: ....

1. Work in a team with your friends. Find out how many of each of the following books are in your classroom:

picture books		poetry books	
plays		stories with no pictures	
information books		atlases	
dictionaries		thesauruses	

2. Do you think there are enough books to suit everyone's differing reading ability?

3. If your teacher had some money to buy more books what would you recommend that he/she buy? Why?

4. Do you have any stories to listen to through headphones?

5. Do you have access to reading material on a computer?

6. Do you have any displays about reading?

7. Do you like them?

18. Bianca's beans (1)

Aim

The children will read the first chapter of a story and discuss the main character. They will look at the dialogue, the action and the descriptions, and discuss what they tell us about the characters. They will decide whether they think it is a good story opening or not, and compare it with other stories they have read.

Activities

The children should listen while the teacher reads the story excerpt on sheet **17a**.

Ask them about their first impressions of Bianca, why she might be so angry and who they think might be to blame for this. Who do they think the old woman is?

Hand out copies of the story to the class. Choose some children for the parts of Bianca, the old woman and the narrator and have them read the story again twice. Ask the children to work in groups to complete the questions on page **17b**. Give help to the less able children where needed. The more able children could write a paragraph or two about what they think might happen next.

Plenary

Bring the class together again and discuss the answers to the worksheet. Hear the written answers to what they think might happen next in the story and encourage others to give an opinion as well.

Discuss how the story begins (with speech and action straight away). Did they think that this was a good opening for a story or not? Why? Would they like to find out what happens next? How does this opening compare to those of other stories they have read?

Bianca's beans (1)

"They'll pay for this!" Bianca shouted. "Rotten lot!" she roared as she stomped across the park. She sat down on the edge of a bench with such a thump that the old lady on the other end shot up into the air. Bianca didn't even notice.

"They can't do this to me," she screamed and pummelled her fists on the bench. The old lady bounced up and down.

"… cup of tea?"

Bianca turned to look. Her eyes nearly popped out of her head. She had never seen anything like it. She might have said that this old lady's clothes were old-fashioned but these clothes had never been in any kind of fashion.

The threadbare coat which reached to the woman's ankles was black with spotty lumps all over it. Bianca wasn't sure if the lumps were meant to be there or if they were blobs of jam or spaghetti or cat food.

She wore a black hat with stringy purple feathers. Her hair poking out from the sides looked just like the grey, metal pot scrubbers Bianca's Mum used. Her pointed chin bent upwards to meet a spotty, hooked nose and in between long, yellow teeth were bared in a kind of smile.

"Can you spare some coins for a cup of tea?" she asked in a shaky voice. Bianca snorted and then roared, "No! Go away and stop bothering me."

"I'll give you something in exchange."

"What?" Bianca asked greedily. "What will you give me?"

Extract by May Stevenson

Bianca's beans (1)

Name: ....

1. How does the author show us that Bianca is becoming more and more angry?

2. Who do you think Bianca might be angry at?

3. What do you think they might have done to make her so angry?

4. What is your first impression of Bianca?

5. What words or phrases made you feel this way?

6. Perhaps Bianca has good reason to be angry at someone, but what tells us that she isn't a very nice character anyway?

7. Discuss in your group what you think the old lady might give Bianca in exchange for the price of a cup of tea.

Extension activity
Continue the story in your own words.

19. Bianca's beans (2)

Aim

The children will read an extract from a story, and discuss the characters and how they feel about them. They will compare this extract with other stories they have read. Then they will re-write the story as a play script.

Activities

Hand out copies of sheet **19a** to the class. Choose children to read the parts of Bianca, the old lady and the narrator and ask them to read the story aloud. Choose other children to read the story again.

Ask the children how they feel about Bianca and what in the story makes them think this way. Who do they think the old lady might be? Why do they think she disappeared? What new things do we learn about the characters in this part of the story? Do we learn this from what they say or what they do? Encourage as many children as possible to take part in the discussion.

Ask the children to complete sheet **19b**, giving help where needed.

Plenary

Bring the class together again and discuss answers to the worksheet. Ask if they have ever encountered behaviour like Bianca's in real life or in another story they have read. Discuss the answers to the questions and hear any endings to the story that have been written. Discuss these.

Extension activity

Revise play script layouts. Ask the children to write out either of the two sections they have read of "Bianca's Beans" as a play script. More able children can do both sections. Perform.

Bianca's beans (2)

The old lady's thin fingers poked around in her bag and produced a bracelet. Bianca went to grab it from her and then pulled her hand back.

"That's made of old, dry beans!" she shouted.

"They are magic beans," the old lady said with a smile.

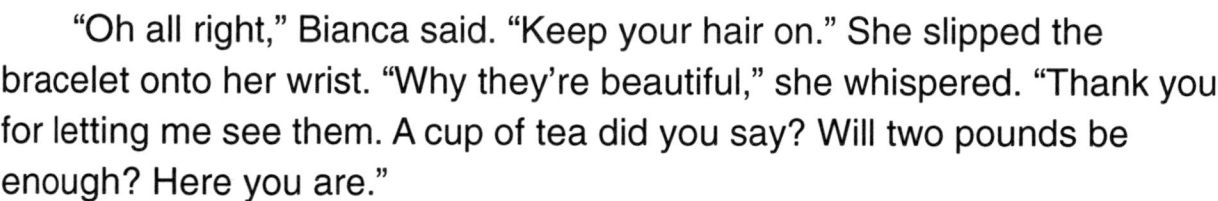

"Oh yeah, right! Oh cool! I'm supposed to believe that? Yeah, right on. Do you think my name's Jack, as in Beanstalk Jack? Get lost and take your stupid beans with you. I'm not giving you a penny."

"You really need them my dear," the old woman said with a gentle smile. "Just hold the bracelet for a second."

"Oh all right," Bianca said. "Keep your hair on." She slipped the bracelet onto her wrist. "Why they're beautiful," she whispered. "Thank you for letting me see them. A cup of tea did you say? Will two pounds be enough? Here you are."

She handed the money over and looked down again at the beans. "They really are nice," she murmured and turned to the old woman. She had vanished. Bianca looked all around, even underneath the bench but she had disappeared completely.

"Oh well," she said to herself. "Now where was I? Oh yes, I was going to meet the others but they didn't show up. Oh, I expect something important came up. I can always see them another day."

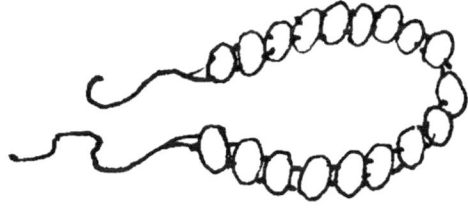

She smiled to herself and walked quietly through the park. As she went, she slipped the bracelet off her wrist and put it into her bag for safe keeping.

Extract by May Stevenson

Bianca's beans (2)

Name: ....

1. When the old woman tells Bianca the beans are magic, how does Bianca react?

2. The old lady tells Bianca that she really needs the beans. What do you think she believes the beans might do for Bianca?

3. What happens when Bianca wears the bracelet?

4. What has happened to the old lady when Bianca turns to speak to her?

5. Why does Bianca slip the bracelet into her bag?

6. Write an ending to the story. You can use the back of the sheet if you need to.

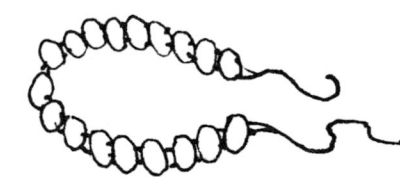

20. Story openings

Aim

The children will compare a number of story beginnings from nineteenth-century and modern texts, and decide what makes a good opening. They will observe how action and words can both help to draw a character. They will decide whether a book appeals by observing details in the text.

Activities

You will need to have available a wide selection of modern children's literature. Ask the children to talk about a book which they have read and enjoyed. How did it begin? Did the opening appeal to them? Was the ending as good as they thought it would be?

Give the children sheet **20a** and let them read the first extract. Ask for opinions as to what might have happened to Marley and whether they would want to read on. Do the same with the other extracts, asking what we learn about the characters or the speaker, and what they think the book will be about.

Hand out sheet **20b** and ask the children to complete the questions, helping the less able children where necessary. The more able children can complete the extension activity to challenge them further.

Plenary

As a whole class discuss the answers to questions 1 and 2, taking as many answers as possible. Remind the children that these books were the equivalent of television, cinema or computers to children of that era. Ask who their favourite modern authors are and why. Make a list of modern story openings and display it to encourage reading.

Story openings

1 Marley was dead: to begin with. There is no doubt whatever about that.
Old Marley was as dead as a door-nail.

from A Christmas Carol *by Charles Dickens (1812–1870)*

2 Squire Trelawney, Dr. Livesey, and the rest of these gentlemen having asked me to write down the whole particulars about Treasure Island, from the beginning to the end, keeping nothing back but the bearings of the island, and that only because there is still treasure not yet lifted, I take up my pen in the year of grace 17--, and go back to the time when my father kept the Admiral Benbow inn, and the brown old seaman with the sabre cut first took up his lodging under our roof.

from Treasure Island *by Robert Louis Stevenson (1850–1894)*

3 "Christmas won't be Christmas without any presents," grumbled Jo, lying on the rug.
"It's so dreadful to be poor!" sighed Meg, looking down at her old dress.

from Little Women *by Louisa May Alcott (1832–1888)*

4 I will begin the story of my adventures with a certain morning early in the month of June, the year of grace 1751, when I took the key for the last time out of the door of my father's house.

from Kidnapped *by Robert Louis Stevenson (1850–1894)*

Story openings

Name: ....

1. Which of these story openings would be most likely to make you want to read the rest of the book, or at least to find out what happens next?

2. Which one might put you off the book?

3. Which of the openings tells you most about what is to follow?

4. Which one tells you least about the book?

5. Find a modern book which you have **not** read before and which has an opening which makes you want to read on. Write down the opening few lines.

6. Write down why you think you would want to read the rest of this book.

7. Choose a book which you have read and enjoyed. Write down the opening few sentences and then say what made you think that the book would be good.

8. Was the book as good as you thought it would be? Give a reason for your answer.

Extension activity

Write your own story opening for the title "Treasure Island".

21. Lorelei

Aim

The children will read a traditional German myth and look for the moral or message in it. They will find examples of descriptive and metaphorical language, and compare this myth with other myths, legends or fables, identifying similar features in them.

Activities

Read the story of Lorelei to the class and discuss it with them. Why might this story be told to sailors? (To make them stay away from the treacherous rock in the river. Never to jilt a fiancée!)

Hand out sheet **21a** and ask the children to take turns at reading part of the story out loud, until they understand it. Ask the children to find examples of descriptive language, such as "swirling water", "long, golden hair", "silvery, whispery sound", "made the river boil" or "great, towering waves".

The children should then answer the questions on sheet **21b**. Help may be needed for the less able children. Give the more able copies of other fables (e.g. Aesop's Fables) to complete the extension activity.

Plenary

Bring the children together again as a class and discuss the answers. Ask if they know of any other fables and compare them. Let them discuss why fables came about (usually as warnings).

Lorelei

A long time ago, so the story goes, a young girl called Lorelei was about to be married. Then the young man she loved dearly married another girl instead.

Lorelei was so heart-broken that she no longer wanted to live. She climbed to the top of a large rock which sticks out into the river Rhine, and threw herself into the swirling water and drowned.

She was turned into a lovely water nymph with a beautiful voice. Every evening at sunset, Lorelei appeared on the rock combing her long, golden hair and singing sweet songs.

She hated all men now, and knew that the silvery, whispery sound of her voice would attract sailors to the rock, where their boats would be wrecked and they would drown.

Many sailors were lured to their deaths until a young man decided to do something about it. He and some friends climbed the rock with their ears padded so that they would not be distracted by the sound of Lorelei's voice.

As they approached her, Lorelei knew that she was defeated. She created a violent storm which made the river boil and sent great, towering waves crashing over the rock, but still the men held on. Rather than be captured, Lorelei threw herself into the river, where she drowned and disappeared for ever.

For many years afterwards, sailors still took great care when passing the rock, and so no more were drowned there.

Lorelei

Name: ....

1. Why was Lorelei so unhappy?

2. What did she become after she died?

3. What made the sailors sail too near the rock?

4. What happened to them when they did?

5. Can you think of another reason why boats were wrecked near the large rock?

6. The whispery, musical sound could have been caused by something else. Can you think what?

7. What caused the water nymph to disappear for ever?

8. Why do you think people came to believe the story of Lorelei?

9. This story sends a message to young men. What is it?

10. The story says that the river boiled. What does this mean?

Extension activity

Read some more myths or fables. Is there a message for the reader in them?

22. The story of King Midas

Aim

The children will look a fable from ancient Greece and identify the moral in it. They will note the differences in culture to our own.

Activities

Read the story to the children and ask why Midas wanted more gold and what happened to him as a result. Distribute sheet **22a** and ask the children to take turns at reading aloud a few sentences of the story. Ask what Midas shouted when he realized he could turn things into gold. What two things did Midas think would happen to him if he jumped into the river? Why did he eventually do this anyway? What happened when he jumped into the river? Do they think Midas would still be greedy? Why?

Ask the children to complete sheet **22b**.

As an extension activity, find another copy of the King Midas story (many are available online). Ask the more able children to write a list of similarities and differences on sheet **22c**. Meanwhile the less able could re-write the story as a comic strip using speech bubbles.

Plenary

Ask a few children to recount the story again as far as they can remember. Ask others what they think the moral of the tale was. What in the story tells us that this myth is from another culture? How do we know King Midas would be more careful in future?

The story of King Midas

Once there was a king called Midas, who was very rich. He was also greedy and wanted to be even more wealthy, so he prayed to his gods for more gold.

When he had finished praying, Midas picked up a plate and found that it had turned to solid gold! He touched a vase of flowers and a harp, which both became gold as well.

"I'll be the richest man in the world!" he cried, turning everything around him in his palace into gold. His beautiful, young daughter heard him shouting and came running in. Midas was suddenly afraid to touch her, but she gave him a hug. To his horror, the child became a solid gold statue.

He was so shocked that he reached for a glass of water. The glass and the water became gold and Midas couldn't drink. Then he realized that any food he touched would turn to gold too. He was going to starve to death!

He fell to his knees and prayed to the gods for help.

"Take your daughter and throw yourselves in the river," the gods said.

"But we'll both drown!" Midas wailed. "No we won't," he cried when he thought about it, "the water will become solid gold and crush us to death!"

There was no answer from the gods. Midas had no choice. For the sake of trying to save his daughter he had to do as he was told. He threw himself and his child statue into the river.

The spell was broken. Midas and his daughter were saved. He could no longer turn things into gold, but he no longer wanted to. He had learned his lesson.

The story of King Midas

Name: ....

1. When did Midas realize that he had been a fool?

2. Why did the gods give him the power to turn everything to gold?

3. What lesson do you think Midas learned?

4. Do you think Midas was a very intelligent man? Say why.

5. If someone today is said to have "the Midas touch" it does not mean that that person can turn things into gold. What do you think it means?

The story of King Midas

Name: ....

1. What are the similarities and differences between the two versions of the King Midas story?

Similarities	Differences

2. Is the message the same in both versions?

3. Why do you think there are variations between different versions of the same story (book or film)?

23. Poetry challenge

Aim

The children will read lots of different poetry, and produce a poetry display for the wall. The less able readers will choose their favourite poem to review. The more able will review a narrative poem, noting how it differs from other forms of poetry.

Activities

Make sure you have collected lots of poetry books from around the school or from the local library service. Have the books in the classroom and during the preceding week ask children to read them in reading time or spare moments. For this particular activity split the books so that the less able readers have access to poems at their level and the more able have access to narrative poems. You may also find copies to print out from the internet. Have these ready for this session.

Explain to the children that one group is going to explore narrative poetry. What is a narrative poem? Discuss. They will need to read narrative poems from your resource collection. After about 20 minutes of reading ask this group to copy out their favourite narrative poem as neatly as possible and write a review of it.

The less able group should choose their favourite poem to copy out, and write about why they like it. Sheet **23a** may be used if necessary.

Plenary

Ask the children to read their poems. Discuss what they liked about them. What did the more able group like about narrative poems? How are they different from other poems? Can the children group poems in any way to make a class book (ie. shape poems, rap poems, etc.)?

Mount some poems for a wall display and let the children enjoy their work!

My favourite poem

Name: ....

Title: _____

Written by: _____

(write out the poem in the space below)

I like this poem because: _____

_____

_____

_____

_____

24. Haunted

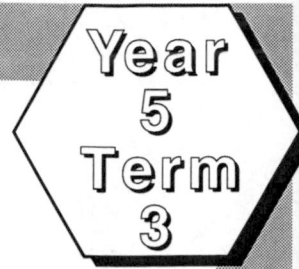

Aim

The children will read an excerpt from a story and then retell and continue it from the point of view of one of the characters.

Activities

Read the extract, then hand out sheet **24a** and ask the children to read it for themselves. Ask why the boys thought the cottage might be haunted in the first place. What did they find creepy? Ask what the children think the boys would do when they heard the screaming. Ask for opinions as to what might have caused the screaming.

Ask the children to read the passage again and then re-write and continue the story from Conner's point of view on sheet **24b**. Tell them that he really believes there is a ghost in the cottage.

Plenary

Ask the children to read their stories and give comments on them. If there is time the children could discuss other scary stories they have read.

Haunted

The boys had been warned countless times not to go near the ruined cottage in the woods. Some people said it was haunted. Rubbish!

They pushed aside some bramble bushes and there it was. All the windows had been smashed and cobwebs hung thickly from the shards of glass. The doorway was just a gaping hole. Part of the roof had fallen in and wasps were buzzing around the remains of a chimney. It was creepy all right, but haunted?

Jack gave a nervous laugh, trying to sound brave. He sauntered up to the doorway and peered in, while Conner stood watching him.

"See – there's nothing to be afraid of!" Jack said. "Come on, let's go inside."

It was then that the screaming began.

Extract by May Stevenson

Haunted

Name: ....

Re-write the story on sheet 24a from Conner's point of view. He definitely believes that the cottage is haunted. Continue the story.

25. Older stories

Aim

The children will read two extracts from nineteenth century literature and discuss the language used, and any archaic words or phrases.

Activities

Explain to the children that as time goes by, fashions in literature change, just as fashions in clothes or hairstyles do. Point out that in a busy world, words in stories become simpler as people take less time to read. In the past, people liked to read long and exciting descriptions in stories.

Hand out sheet **25a** and read the first excerpt to the class, explaining any words or phrases the children are unsure about. What does the author mean by "give a little sketch"?

Read the second excerpt on sheet **25a** to the children and talk about it before reading it again. Ask the children which words they did not understand and write them on the board. Ask the children to find their meaning in a dictionary. Is there any humour in this extract?

Give the less able children sheet **25b** and a dictionary, and ask them to complete it.

Ask the more able children to work in groups on sheet **25c**.

Plenary

Bring the children together again and discuss the words they have chosen, explaining anything they don't understand.

Ask the children for any words they hear their grandparents use that they find odd or that they don't understand. Discuss these as a class.

Older stories

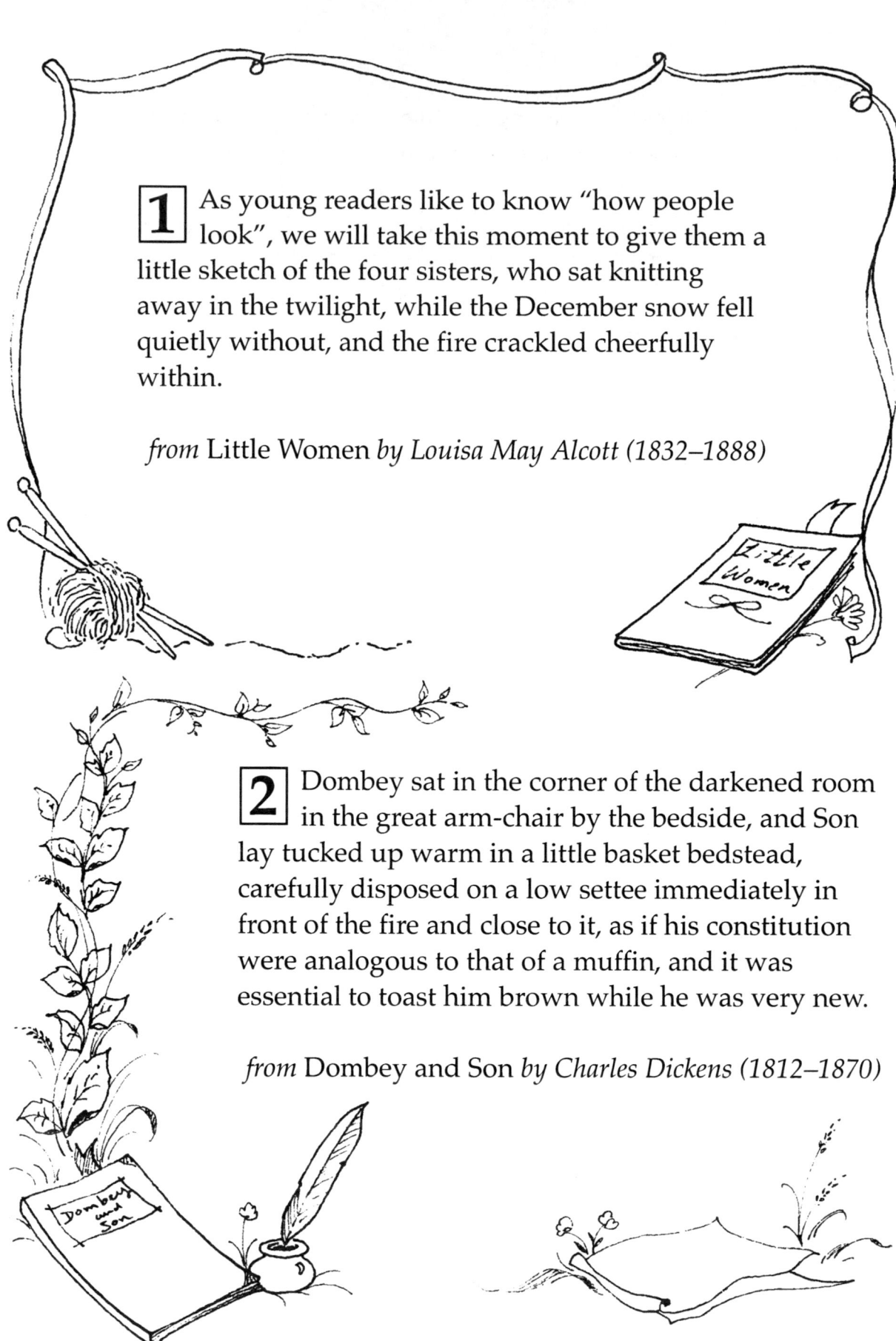

1 As young readers like to know "how people look", we will take this moment to give them a little sketch of the four sisters, who sat knitting away in the twilight, while the December snow fell quietly without, and the fire crackled cheerfully within.

from Little Women *by Louisa May Alcott (1832–1888)*

2 Dombey sat in the corner of the darkened room in the great arm-chair by the bedside, and Son lay tucked up warm in a little basket bedstead, carefully disposed on a low settee immediately in front of the fire and close to it, as if his constitution were analogous to that of a muffin, and it was essential to toast him brown while he was very new.

from Dombey and Son *by Charles Dickens (1812–1870)*

Dictionary challenge

Name: ....

Look up these words from the text in a dictionary. Write down what they mean.

1. twilight
2. bedstead
3. constitution
4. analogous
5. muffin
6. essential

Older stories

Name: ....

Read the two extracts again. Working in a group, answer the following questions:

1. Look up any words or phrases that you did not understand and write their definitions below:

2. Discuss the differences between these passages and passages from modern books.

3. Read the two extracts again for yourself. Did they mean more this time?

4. These stories were written more than one hundred years ago, but language is still changing. Do your grandparents use any words or phrases that you don't understand? Discuss with your group.

5. List some old-fashioned phrases which you have heard below, for example, "burning the midnight oil" (meaning "working late into the night"):

26. Let's talk about books

Aim

The children will be encouraged to talk about what books they enjoy reading. They will be aware of established authors and the types of books they write, and discuss the wide range of themes covered in fiction books. They will be aware of and respond to the views of others.

Activities

Ask the children which books they are reading at present and invite them to talk about what they think of the story, the characters, etc., what they think is special about that author's work and how it compares with other authors they have read. Make a note on the board of each author and title of the book mentioned, then make a list on the board of various themes in literature, such as bullying, loneliness, magic, aggression, poverty, success, etc. Ask for more examples of these themes.

Ask the children to comment on any books they have read which have these themes. Encourage discussion on each of these comments.

Ask the children to complete worksheet **26a** on their own, to elicit opinions from the more shy children who perhaps did not contribute orally.

Plenary

Hear as many as possible of the answers to the worksheet and if necessary add new names on the board. The children should be given a list of these authors and themes to keep.

Extension activity

The more able children could find out how many books in the room are about "bullying", and make a list of the titles and authors.

Let's talk about books

Name: ....

1. Write down the title of a book which you have read recently.

2. Did you enjoy it? Why?

3. Which kind of book do you like best? (For example, horror, adventure, magic, school stories, sport stories, funny stories, animal stories, etc.) You can choose more than one type. Maybe your type is not here. If not, write it down.

4. Who is your favourite author? Why?

5. Where do you read most? (In bed? In school? Outside? At home?)

6. If you met your favourite author, what would you ask him/her?

7. If you could write a book, what would it be about?

8. Have a discussion in your group about literature that you like. Perhaps you can persuade your friends to read books by your favourite author.

27. Book or film?

Aim

The children will discuss the differences between books and their television or film versions. They will be encouraged to say what is special about authors they like and how the text of some books affects them. They will listen to the views of each other, respond to them and build on them.

Activities

Ask the children for the titles of books they have read recently which have also been made into films or television programmes and put these on the board. Choose one book and ask all of the children who have read it to comment on it. Were there differences between the two versions? Were the characters and settings in the screen version the way they imagined them in the book? Did it follow the plot of the book accurately? Which did they enjoy more? Ask for reasons. Do the same with other books until as many children as possible have made a contribution.

Ask the children for names of their favourite authors and put them on the board. Ask for opinions about these authors considering their styles and themes. How did the authors' books make the pupils feel when they read them?

Arrange the children in small groups and ask them to complete the questions on sheet **27a**.

Plenary

As a class, give as many children as possible a chance to answer some of questions 1–7. Then ask for volunteers who have done the extension activity to read out their story, asking for comments from other children.

Book or film?

Name: ....

1. Choose a book you have read which has been made into a television programme or film that you have seen, and write down the title.

2. Which did you enjoy more, the book or the screen version?

3. Did the screen version follow the story accurately or did it change things?

4. How were the characters different to the way you had imagined them in the book?

5. How were the settings different to the way you had imagined them in?

6. Which did you prefer, the way the author described characters and settings, or the way they were in the screen version?

7. Think of your favourite author. What is special about his/her work?

8. With a partner, take it in turns to read out your answers to each question and compare and discuss the answers.

Extension activity

Think of a main character in a book who is a hero, or "goodie". Think of a character who is a villain, or "baddie". Try telling part of the story from the point of view of the "baddie".

28. From a railway carriage

Aim

The children will look at a poem from the nineteenth century and look for rhyme, alliteration and words that create a sense of speed. They will also see how the poet uses specially chosen words to create vivid pictures, to produce the rhythm he wants and to convey excitement.

Activities

Give each child a copy of sheet **28a** and read the poem to them. Let the children read it out loud as a class. Can they find pairs of rhyming words?

Ask them what were "faster than fairies". What were "charging along like troops"? What did the speaker see "whistle by"? Were these things really moving?

What was the child gathering? What was the tramp doing? What is meant by "stringing the daisies"? What happened to the cart? What happened to all the things outside the train? Did the children find it easy to picture these things?

When these questions are answered, ask the children to read the poem along with you, trying to find the rhythm of the train. How do they think the poet felt in the train? Why? Ask the children to work out how long ago it is since Robert Louis Stevenson was born and find out if they know of any other authors or poets of that era.

The less able children can complete sheet **28b**. Give help where needed.

Ask the more able children to complete sheet **28c** as far as they are able in the time allowed. Those who finish early can write their own poem about travelling in something, trying to create a sense of its rhythm.

Plenary

Ask different children to read out answers to their exercise and compare and discuss with the class. Ask the children what they liked or disliked about the poem. Hear any poems the children may have written.

From a railway carriage

Faster than fairies, faster than witches,
Bridges and houses, hedges and ditches;
And charging along like troops in a battle,
All through the meadows the horses and cattle:
All of the sights of the hill and the plain
Fly as thick as driving rain;
And ever again, in the wink of an eye,
Painted stations whistle by.

Here is a child who clambers and scrambles,
All by himself and gathering brambles;
Here is a tramp who stands and gazes;
And there is the green for stringing the daisies!
Here is a cart run away in the road
Lumping along with man and load;
And here is a mill and there is a river:
Each a glimpse and gone for ever!

Robert Louis Stevenson (1850–1894)

From a railway carriage

Name: ....

1. What tells us which season of the year it is?

2. What is a "tramp"?

3. Was the tramp in a hurry? What tells us this?

4. The poet uses alliteration in the poem (using the same sound at the beginning of words close to each other), for example, "Faster than fairies". Write down any other examples of this in the poem.

5. Make a list of all the words or phrases which help to create a sense of speed.

6. Look at the date of birth of the poet. What does this tell us about the train?

From a railway carriage

Name: ....

In a group, take turns at reading the first verse aloud, trying to read it as a single sentence. You should be able to hear and feel the rhythm of a train. Then work on your own to answer the following questions:

1. Where is the poet when he is writing this poem?

2. The poet talks about "All of the sights of the hill and the plain." Write down what these sights are.

3. What tells us which season of the year it is?

4. What is a "tramp"?

5. Was the tramp in a hurry? What tells us this?

6. The poet uses alliteration in the poem (using the same sound at the beginning of words close to each other), for example, "Faster than fairies". Write down any other examples of this in the poem.

7. Make a list of all the words or phrases which help to create a sense of speed.

8. The poet says "Painted stations whistle by" and "Each a glimpse and gone for ever!" What does this tell us about the train?

9. Look at the date of birth of the poet. What does this tell us about the train?

29. Nonsense poems

Aim

The children will read several nonsense poems and note which words are made up by the poet and which situations are ridiculous, but funny. They will read the poems for themselves, identify rhyming couplets and choose which poem they find the most appealing.

Activities

Hand out sheet **29a**. Read "The two old bachelors" to the class and then ask them to read it aloud as a class. What is a bachelor? What were the bachelors going to have for dinner? What would have happened to them if they hadn't had any dinner? Which words rhyme in the poem? What did the children find amusing or ridiculous about the poem?

Do the same with "The courtship of the Yonghy-Bonghy-Bo", allowing as many groups of children as possible to take part in reading it aloud. Where did the Yonghy-Bonghy-Bo live? What does "worldly goods" mean? What were his worldly goods? Which words rhyme in the poem? Which lines are ridiculous?

Hand out sheet **29b**. Read "Mr and Mrs Spikky Sparrow" and "The Jumblies" with the children. Discuss these as a class in a similar way.

Hand out sheet **29c** and ask the children to complete the questions. The less able are just to do questions 3 and 4.

Plenary

Ask groups of children to read the poems aloud again. Take a vote on which poem the class liked the most and ask why. Do the same with the poem they liked the least.

Nonsense poems

by Edward Lear (1812–1888)

The two old Bachelors

Two old Bachelors were living in one house;
One caught a Muffin, the other caught a Mouse.
Said he who caught the Muffin to him who caught the Mouse, –
"This happens just in time! For we've nothing in the house,
"Save a tiny slice of lemon and a teaspoonful of honey,
"And what to do for dinner – since we haven't any money?
"And what can we expect if we haven't any dinner,
"But to lose our teeth and eyelashes and keep on growing thinner?"

The courtship of the Yonghy-Bonghy-Bo

On the Coast of Coromandel
  Where the early pumpkins blow,
    In the middle of the woods
    Lived the Yonghy-Bonghy-Bo.
Two old chairs, and half a candle,
One old jug without a handle,
    These were all his worldly goods:
    In the middle of the woods,
    These were all the worldly goods,
  Of the Yonghy-Bonghy-Bo,
  Of the Yonghy-Bonghy-Bo.

Nonsense poems

by Edward Lear (1812–1888)

Mr and Mrs Spikky Sparrow

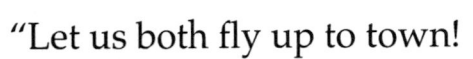

On a little piece of wood,
Mr Spikky Sparrow stood;
Mrs Sparrow sat close by,
A-making of an insect pie,
For her little children five,
In the nest and all alive,
Singing with a cheerful smile
To amuse them all the while,
  "Twikky wikky wikky wee
  "Wikky bikky twikky tee,
  "Spikky bikky bee!"

"Let us both fly up to town!
"There I'll buy you such a gown!
"Which, completely in the fashion,
"You shall tie a sky-blue sash on.
"And a pair of slippers neat,
"To fit your darling little feet,
"So that you will look and feel,
"Quite galloobious and genteel!
  "Jikky wikky bikky see,
  "Chicky bikky wikky bee,
  "Twicky witchy wee!"

The Jumblies

They went to sea in a Sieve, they did,
In a Sieve they went to sea:
In spite of all their friends could say,
On a winter's morn, on a stormy day,
In a Sieve they went to sea!

Nonsense poems

Name: ....

Take it in turns to read verses of the poems. Then answer the following questions:

1. What did you like best about the poems?

2. These poems are very old. Why do you think people still enjoy them?

3. Write down all the nonsense words and phrases that you can find in the poems.

4. Make up some nonsense words of your own and try to write a poem using them.

30. Taking sides

Aim

The children will understand why an author divides the text into paragraphs when writing a story. They will also think about the feelings of a character and discuss the topic of bullying.

Activities

Read the passage to the children. Hand out sheet **30a** and ask a child to read the first paragraph. Discuss it with the class, asking questions to check the children have understood it. Do the same with the other paragraphs.

Ask why the writer has divided the text into paragraphs. Get the children to notice what changes between the paragraphs, such as the location or what a character is thinking about.

Discuss the dilemma that Sam is in. What do the children think Sam should do? What stops him from doing certain things? What might happen if he told on Mickey? Ask the children to read the passage again before they complete the question sheets. Make sure they know the meaning of words like "furtively", "emerged" or "sauntered".

Give sheet **30b** to the less able children and give them help, discussing some questions with them before they attempt an answer. More able children are to complete sheet **30c**.

Plenary

Ask the questions orally and hear as many answers as possible. Ask the children if they have read any books about bullying and ask for their opinions on them.

Taking sides

Sam's mind was made up. He had to keep a close watch on his friend Gary. Surely things would get better? Surely Mickey would get fed up with bullying Gary and him? He suddenly felt a twinge of guilt as he realized that he was wishing that Mickey and his gang would find some other poor victim to bully.

Saturday came and Sam decided to go into town and keep a look-out. He hoped he wouldn't see Gary at all, but his hopes were dashed. There Gary was, looking in a shop window and glancing furtively around him.

A few minutes later he disappeared into the newsagent's. After about five minutes he emerged, his jacket zipped up to the neck. Sam followed him, knowing what he would do. Sure enough, Gary sauntered a little way down the high street and then he ran.

Sam didn't bother to chase after him. He felt utterly miserable. So his friend was still stealing? Maybe Mickey wasn't making him do it after all. Maybe Gary just liked stealing.

What should he do? Should he tell the police so that they could sort Gary's problem out? But what if they sent him away, or something worse? But if he did nothing, where would it end for Gary? Where would it end for himself, because he knew about the shoplifting and let it carry on?

Sam was afraid of what his mum would say if she knew he was involved. He was also afraid of what it would do to Gary's sick mother if she found out her son was a thief. It was an impossible situation.

Extract by May Stevenson

Taking sides

Name: ....

1. Read the first paragraph of the story. How is Sam feeling? Who is bullying Sam and Gary?

2. Why does Sam feel guilty about wishing that Mickey would stop bullying them?

3. What is Mickey making Gary do?

4. Read the fourth paragraph. How is Sam feeling now? If he knows that Gary is shoplifting, what should Sam do about it?

5. What are Sam's thoughts in paragraph five? Why doesn't he report Gary to the police?

© May Stevenson

This page may be photocopied for use by the purchasing institution only.

Brilliant Activities for Reading Fiction

107

Taking sides

Name: ....

1. Read the first paragraph of the story. How is Sam feeling? Who is bullying Sam and Gary?

2. Why does Sam feel guilty about wishing that Mickey would stop bullying them?

3. What is Mickey making Gary do?

4. Read the fourth paragraph. How is Sam feeling now? If Sam knows that Gary is shoplifting, what should he do about it?

5. What are Sam's thoughts in paragraph five? Why doesn't he report Gary to the police?

6. The author starts a new paragraph each time to tell us about Sam's feelings. What does he feel in the last paragraph? Should the boys tell their parents about the situation?

7. What could Sam and Gary do to stop Mickey from bullying them?

8. What do you think might happen to them if they reported Mickey?

9. What do you think might eventually happen to Gary if Sam allows him to go on stealing for Mickey?

Extension activity

Try to find a book which contains bullying and read it for yourself.

31. Flower poems

Aim

The children will read two poems of a similar theme by the same author. They will look at the personification of a flower, rhyme and alliteration. They will discuss the similarities and differences between the poems and whether these indicate that they could be written by the same poet.

Activities

Hand out sheet **31a** and read the first poem, "Daffodowndilly". Discuss as a class what the poem is about. How is the daffodil like a person? Does this poem rhyme? Are there any examples of alliteration?

Read the second poem, "Water-lilies". Discuss as a class what the poem is about? Who might the Lake King's daughter be? Is she real or imaginary? Does this poem rhyme? Are there any examples of alliteration?

Do the children think that the poems are written by the same person? Why? Discuss style, language, etc. They are both written by A.A. Milne (1882–1956).

Split the children into two groups. The less able children will focus on the first poem only and complete sheet **31b**. The more able will look at both poems and complete sheet **31c**. As an extension activity the more able could find other poems about flowers, and look at the similarities and differences.

Plenary

Discuss the children's answers. Did they like these poems or not? Which one did they prefer? Why? Hear the poems that the children have written.

Flower poems

Daffodowndilly

She wore her yellow sun-bonnet,
   She wore her greenest gown;
She turned to the south wind
   And curtsied up and down.
She turned to the sunlight
   And shook her yellow head,
And whispered to her neighbour:
   "Winter is dead."

Water-lilies

Where the water-lilies go
To and fro,
Rocking in the ripples of the water,
Lazy on a leaf lies the Lake King's daughter,
And the faint winds shake her.
Who will come and take her?
I will! I will!
Keep still! Keep still!
Sleeping on a leaf lies the Lake King's daughter …
Then the wind comes skipping
To the lilies on the water;
And the kind winds wake her.
Now who will take her?
With a laugh she is slipping
Through the lilies on the water.
Wait! Wait!
Too late! Too late!
Only the water-lilies go
To and fro,
Dipping, dipping,
To the ripples of the water.

From *When We Were Very Young* by A.A. Milne © The Trustees of the Pooh Properties. Published by Egmont UK Ltd London and used with permission.

Flower poems

Name: ....

1. Read "Daffodowndilly" again. What flower is the poem about?

2. Which part of the flower is "her yellow sun-bonnet"?

3. Which part of the flower is "her greenest gown"?

4. Who is her neighbour?

5. Why do you think they would be pleased that "Winter is dead"?

6. Think of another plant. It could be a different flower (eg. a rose, a tulip or a daisy) or it could be a tree, or even a weed! Write your own poem about that plant, making it sound like a real person, if you can. What is the plant wearing or doing?

Flower poems

Name: ....

1. Read both poems again and fill in the chart:

	Daffodowndilly	Water-lilies
a) Does the poem rhyme? Underline any rhyming words.		
b) Does the poem have alliteration? Circle any examples.		
c) What is the poem about?		
d) Do you think the author has a good imagination? Why?		
e) Is the poem modern? Which words indicate this?		

2. Why do you think the poet makes the daffodil like a real person in "Daffodowndilly"?

3. Is the second poem more about water-lilies or the Lake King's daughter?

4. What do you think the Lake King's daughter is? Why?

5. Are there any reasons that you can tell the two poems are written by the same poet? Give examples.

6. Write your own poem about a plant, which has an imaginary creature living in, on or near it.

32. Robert Louis Stevenson

Aim

The children will read several poems by the same poet and discuss the themes running through them. They will discuss the poet's imagination and the style appropriate for children. They will find rhyming words in each poem and note any archaic words or phrases.

Activities

Divide the class into four mixed ability groups. Hand out sheet **32a** and ask each group to read a poem out loud. Then swap the poems until every child has read at least two poems. Ask the children if they can see similar themes in the poems, such as travel, or loneliness and being confined to the house through sickness. Ask for specific phrases in the poems that relate to these themes.

Discuss how the poems talk about the imagination and ask the children for examples of the speaker's imagination in each poem. Why do they think children would enjoy reading these poems? Are they easy to read? Is the language suited to children?

Ask the children to find rhyming words in each poem.

Ask the less able children to answer the questions on sheet **32b** and the more able to complete sheet **32c**. Give help where needed.

The more able children could be asked to write a simple verse in the manner of R.L. Stevenson on loneliness, illness, travel or the imagination.

Plenary

Go over the answers to the worksheets with the children. Ask for opinions of the poems. How does being unwell and staying in bed make them feel? Why it would be harder for a child like R.L. Stevenson to bear?

Hear any poems that the children have written. If possible read more poems from "A Child's Garden Of Verses" by R.L. Stevenson.

Robert Louis Stevenson

1 The land of counterpane

When I was sick and lay a-bed,
I had two pillows at my head,
And all my toys beside me lay
To keep me happy all the day.
I sometimes sent my ships in fleets
All up and down among the sheets;
Or brought my trees and houses out,
And planted cities all about.

2 Travel

I should like to rise and go
Where the golden apples grow; –
Where below another sky
Parrot islands anchored lie,
And, watched by cockatoos and goats,
Lonely Crusoes building boats; –
There I'll come when I'm a man
With a camel caravan.

3 A good play

We built a ship upon the stairs
All made of the back-bedroom chairs,
And filled it full of sofa pillows
To go a-sailing on the billows.

4 The little land

When at home alone I sit
And am very tired of it,
I have just to shut my eyes
To go sailing through the skies –
To go sailing far away
To the pleasant land of play.

Robert Louis Stevenson

Name: ....

1. Robert Louis Stevenson was very ill as a child and spent a lot of time either in bed or confined to the house. Do you think these poems show this? Write down any words or phrases that tell us.

2. What theme runs through all of these poems?

3. Later in life Robert Louis Stevenson travelled a lot to many parts of the world. Which words in the poems tell us that he might do so?

4. Which words tell us that he was probably a very lonely little boy?

5. Robert Louis Stevenson died in 1894. Which words in the poems tell you that they were written a long time ago?

Robert Louis Stevenson

Name: ....

1. Robert Louis Stevenson was very ill as a child and spent a lot of time either in bed or confined to the house. Do you think these poems show this? Write down any words or phrases that tell us.

2. What theme runs through all of these poems?

3. Later in life Robert Louis Stevenson travelled a lot to many parts of the world. Which words or phrases in the poems tell us that he might do so?

4. Which words tell us that he was probably a very lonely little boy?

5. Robert Louis Stevenson died in 1894. Which words in the poems tell you that they were written a long time ago?

6. In "Travel", who is the "Crusoe" he would like to see?

7. What quality do you think Robert Louis Stevenson had to help him through his illness as a child?

8. What is meant by the following phrases?

a) "a camel caravan":

b) "a counterpane":

Answers to worksheets

Year 3 Term 1

1. Fairy tale beginnings

Sheet **1b**:
1. Little Red Riding Hood
2. Goldilocks and the Three Bears
3. Sleeping Beauty
4. Cinderella
5. Pinocchio

Sheets **1c** and **1d**:
1. Goldilocks and the Three Bears
2. Cinderella
3. Sleeping Beauty
4. Pinocchio
5. Little Red Riding Hood

2. Moonshadows

Sheet **2b**:
A 1–4. *open questions*
   5. creep
B 1–2. *open questions*
   3. verse 1: shape, shadow
      verse 2: spidery, spiky; creep, curtains; worried, wee
      verse 3: monsters, making; not, nothing; don't dare
      verse 4: morning, moonlight; forget, fears
      verse 5: pencils, pile
      for rhyme, see line endings
   4. *open question*

3. Heroes don't cry

Sheet **3b**:
1. "hammered on the door", "leaned hard on the bell", "banged on a window"
2. speech marks (inverted commas), new paragraph when new person speaks
3. a) "What if they catch us?"
   b) "Run!"

Sheet **3c**:
1. *see* **3b** *question 1*

2. tangled, overgrown, tall, scowling, bearded, crumbling, evil
3. a–b) *see* **3b** *question 3 a–b)*
   c) "There's two kids", "I'm gonna get them", "We've got to get help"
4. *open question*

Year 3 Term 2

4. Themes in fairy tales

Sheet **4b**:
1. someone with great difficulties winning in the end
2. weak character defeating strong one

Sheet **4c**: *open questions*

5. Story beginnings and endings

Sheets **5a** and **5b**:
   Little Red Riding Hood: 1(**5a**) – 3(**5b**)
   Sleeping Beauty: 2(**5a**) – 1(**5b**)
   Aladdin: 3(**5a**) – 4(**5b**)
   Pinocchio: 4(**5a**) – 2(**5b**)

6. Character study

Sheet **6b**: *open activity*

Year 3 Term 3

7. Jenny on the ginger jar

Sheet **7b**:
1. cold, hazy, soft, frothy-grey
2. swirled, twirled, danced, curled
3. c) the attic
4. *open question*

Sheet **7c**:
1. to try to see more clearly, to wake herself up
2. dust
3. in the attic
4. the darkest corner of the room
5–7. *open questions*

8. Vek's visit

Sheet **8b**:
A 1. gym, "run around the room"
   2. Vek thanks him for everything he has learned
   3. he was going to extract and peel his eye
   4–6. *open questions*

Sheet **8c**:
1. a) hurry up
   b) stop talking
   c) be quick
   d) watch out
2. *open question*

Year 4 Term 1

9. Vek goes to school

Sheet **9b**:
1. her face grew pink
2. she probably felt faint
3. she might die of fright
4. he called out that he felt dizzy
5. she thought he might be the headmaster's nephew
6. *open question*

Sheet **9c**:
1–5. *see sheet* **9b**
6–9. *open questions*

10. Character descriptions

Sheet **10a**:
1. 15
2. no – "very tall", "long limbs"
3. a colt, a young horse
4. grey
5. comical (funny)

Sheet **10b**
1. mean with money
2. *open question*
3. greedy and envious
4. someone who does wrong
5. cold-hearted
6. greedy, miserly
7. the way he walked
8. *open question*

Answers to worksheets

11. The whole truth

Sheet 11c
1. directions written in italics
2. listed under "Characters"
3. speak when name is written
4. they are sitting far apart, Becky looks unhappy
5–6. *open questions*

Year 4 Term 2

12. The lamplighter

Sheet 12b:
1–2. a lamplighter
3. a banker
4. lantern, ladder
5. *see line endings*

Sheet 12c:
1. it has become dark
2. sit at the window
3. going to lampposts one by one and lighting lamps
4. "my papa's a banker and as rich as he can be"
5. "when I am stronger"
6. Tom – driver, Maria – go to sea
7. be a lamplighter
8. wants to be outside, can only see this occupation from window, grown fond of Leerie
9. when he is better and sees other jobs, probably won't be lamplighter; rich, able to choose occupation
10. longs for Leerie to see him and nod to him

13. The creature in the cave

Sheet 13b:
1. cave is lit, walls covered in streamers, stars
2. a) wide as saucers
   b) a kitten
   c) a giant piece of bubble gum
3. to clean it
4. streamers, sparkling stars; creature crawl; blinding blue; cartons, cans

Sheet 13c:
1. walls are decorated with streamers and sparkling stars, soft, shimmering glow is coming from back of cave
2. crawled, slithered
3. as wide as saucers
   as nervous as a kitten
   like a giant piece of bubble gum
4. *see sheet* **13b** *question 4*
5. surprised, frightened
6. *open question*

14. The seasons

Sheet 14b:
1. a) verse 2
   b) verse 1
   c) verse 4
   d) verse 3
2. a) verse 1: meadows, mayflowers, butterflies, bees, children, ice-creams, knees, feet, sand, sea, sand dune
   verse 2: bluebells, lambs, hills, birds, daffodils, chickens, hot cross buns
   verse 3: bells, stars, sky, ice, windows, snow, mince pies, cream, cake, parcels, presents
   verse 4: squirrels, trees, leaves, ground, sparks, bonfire, night, sausages
   b) verse 1: bees, splash, sea
   verse 2: lambs, birds singing, chickens
   verse 3: bells are ringing
   verse 4: sparks, sausages sizzle
   c) verse 1: mayflowers, sea
   verse 2: bluebells, daffodils, hot cross buns
   verse 3: mince pies, cake
   verse 4: bonfire, sausages
   d) verse 1: ice-creams, tea
   verse 2: hot cross buns
   verse 3: mince pies, cream, cake
   verse 4: sausages

e) verse 1: mayflowers, butterflies, bees, ice-creams drip, firm sand, sea
   verse 2: bluebells, lambs, daffodils, silky-soft chickens, fluffy, warm hot cross buns, the cold
   verse 3: ice, snow, mince pies, cream, cake, parcels
   verse 4: leaves, sparks, bonfire, sausages
3. verse 1: meadows, mayflowers; butterflies, bees; feet, firm; sand, splash, sea
   verse 2: singing sweetly; silky-soft
   verse 3: stars, sky; cream, Christmas, cake; parcels, presents
   verse 4: sausages sizzle
4. *see line endings*

Year 4 Term 3

15. Simple verses

Sheet 15b: *see line endings*

Sheet 15c:
1. six, sticks (verse 1); sneeze, sorrow (verse 3); wealthy, wise (verse 4)
2. *see line endings*
3. verse 1: to learn to count up to twenty
   verse 2: to learn the number of days in each month of the year
   verse 3: to learn the days of the week
   verse 4: to encourage child to go to bed early / to get up early
4. *open question*
5. art thou
6. bow, wow, wow, Tommy Tinker
7. to warn child to stay away from unfamiliar dogs; to describe the sound a dog makes and ask the child to repeat it
8. *open question*

Answers to worksheets

16. New neighbours

Sheet **16b**:
1. high unemployment in Poland, Piotr could get better job in England and earn more; his family came to be with him
2. Piotr
3. *open question*
4. they are friendly, kind, interesting
5. yes – he finds out more in books
6. they eat boiled eggs with horseradish sauce; no chocolate eggs
7. *open question*

Sheet **16c**: *open activity*

17. Reading reviews

Sheets **17a** and **17b**: *open activities*

Year 5 Term 1

18. Bianca's beans (1)

Sheet **18b**:
1. shouts, roars, screams; stomps, sits with a thump, pummels bench
2–5. *open questions*
6. shouts at old lady who has nothing to do with cause of anger; "greedily"
7. *open question*

19. Bianca's beans (2)

1. rudely, makes fun of old lady
2. *open question*
3. she becomes kind, polite, generous
4. she has disappeared
5. for safe keeping
6. *open question*

20. Story openings

Sheet **20b**: *open questions*

Year 5 Term 2

21. Lorelei

Sheet **21b**:
1. her sweetheart married another girl
2. water nymph
3. they wanted to get close to sweet singing
4. their boats were wrecked on the rock, they drowned
5. water would be choppy near the large rock and pull boats near to it
6. whispering sound of wind, swirling water
7. she knew she was defeated, but did not want to be captured so she drowned herself
8. many sailors drowned near the rock, people thought had to involve magic; people did not want to admit that the sailors might have been careless in dangerous water
9. be faithful to women; don't be tempted by sweet music
10. the water was so churned up that looked like it was being boiled

22. The story of King Midas

Sheet **22b**:
1. when he tried to eat and drink; when daughter touched him
2. to teach him a lesson
3. there are far more important things in life than being rich
4. he wasn't intelligent enough to realize that everything he touched would turn into gold, including food and daughter
5. successful in making money

Sheet **22c**: *open activity*

23. Poetry challenge

Sheet **23a**: *open activity*

Year 5 Term 3

24. Haunted

Sheet **24b**: *open activity*

25. Older stories

Sheets **25b** and **25c**: *open questions*

Year 6 Term 1

26. Let's talk about books

Sheet **26a**: *open questions*

27. Book or film?

Sheet **27a**: *open questions*

28. From a railway carriage

Sheet **28b**:
1. brambles, daisies – summer
2. homeless person, wanderer
3. no – "stands and gazes"
4. faster, fairies; houses, hedges; run, road; lumping, load; glimpse, gone
5. "faster than fairies", "faster than witches", "charging along", "fly", "in the wink of an eye", "whistle by", "a glimpse and gone forever"
6. poet died more than 100 years ago, must be very old train – stream train

Sheet **28c**:
1. in train / railway carriage
2. bridges, houses, hedges, ditches, meadows, horses, cattle, stations, child, brambles, tramp, the green, daisies, cart, man, mill, river
3–7. *see sheet* **28b** *questions 1–5.*
8. fast; probably express train because passing stations without stopping
9. *see sheet* **28b** *queson 6.*

Answers to worksheets

Year 6 Term 2

29. Nonsense poems

Sheet **29c:**
1. *open question*
2. funny, comical, song-like
3. poem 1: caught a Muffin, lose teeth and eyelashes
   poem 2: Coast of Coromandel, early pumpkins blow, Yonghy-Bonghy-Bo
   poem 3: Spikky, Twikky wikky … bee, galloobious, Jikky wikky … wee
   poem 4: the Jumblies, went to sea in a Sieve
4. *open question*

30. Taking sides

Sheet **30b:**
1. first positive then guilty; wants to look after Gary; Mickey and his gang are bullying them
2. Mickey and his gang would probably bully someone else
3. steal things for him
4. utterly miserable; should tell police if can't make Gary stop
5. worried about consequences

Sheet **30c:**
1–5. *see sheet* **30b**
6. worried about parents' reaction; yes
7. tell police, parents or another adult
8. Mickey might tell his gang to hurt them
9. might be caught by police

Year 6 Term 3

31. Flower poems

Sheet **31b:**
1. daffodil
2. petals
3. leaves, stem
4. another daffodil
5. spring is when daffodils appear
6. *open question*

Sheet **31c:**
1. a) yes – *see line endings*
      yes – *see line endings*
   b) yes – greenest gown; whispered, winter
      yes – where, water-lilies; rocking, ripples; lazy, leaf, lies, Lake; water, winds, wake
   c) daffodil
      Lake King's daughter
   d) yes – daffodil described like person
      yes – Lake King's daughter is imaginary, but easy to visualize
   e) no – "sun-bonnet", "gown", "curtsied"
      no – "Lake King's daughter"
2. easy to picture, makes it more interesting
3. Lake King's daughter
4. fairy; small, dainty, playful – "with a laugh she is slipping through the lilies"
5. similar style, imagination, theme
6. *open question*

32. Robert Louis Stevenson

Sheet **32b:**
1. poem 1: "land of counterpane", "sick and lay a-bed", "pillows at my head", "to keep me happy all the day", "sheets"
   poem 2: "I should like to rise and go"
   poem 3: "stairs" "back-bedroom chairs", "sofa pillows"
   poem 4: "at home alone I sit", "very tired of it"
2. longing to travel
3. poem 2: "I should like to rise and go", "below another sky", "parrot islands", "cockatoos and goats", "Crusoes", "There I'll come when I'm a man", "camel caravan"
   poem 3: "to go a-sailing"
   poem 4: "sailing through the skies", "sailing far away"
4. poem 1: "sick and lay a-bed", "to keep me happy through the day"
   poem 4: "at home alone I sit", "very tired of it"
5. poem 1: counterpane, a-bed
   poem 3: a-sailing

Sheet **32c:**
1–5. *see sheet* **32b**
6. Robinson Crusoe; fellow travellers
7. good imagination; dreams of the future
8. a) line of camels carrying goods
   b) bedspread